CARNIVAL of SOULS

RELIGIOUS CULTS and YOUNG PEOPLE

by Joel A. MacCollam

A CROSSROAD BOOK
THE SEABURY PRESS / NEW YORK

Acknowledgments

In chapter 7, the excerpt from *Snapping: America's Epidemic of Sudden Personality Change* by Flo Conway and Jim Siegelman. Copyright © 1978 by Flo Conway and Jim Siegelman. Reprinted by permission of J. B. Lippincott Company.

In chapters 8 and 9, the excerpts from "Religious Totalism: Gentle and Ungentle Persuasion under the First Amendment" by Richard Delgado is copyright © 1977 by the *Southern California Law Review* and reprinted with their permission.

In chapters 8 and 9, the excerpts from *Deprogramming: Documenting the Issue* are used with the permission of the American Civil Liberties Union.

The excerpts quoted throughout this work from *Missionary and Cult Movements*, published by the Union of American Hebrew Congregations, 838 Fifth Avenue, New York, N.Y. 10021, are used with their permission.

Library of Congress Cataloging in Publication Data

MacCollam, Joel A   1946–
    Carnival of souls.

    "A Crossroad book."
    Bibliography: p.
  1. Church work with young adults—Case studies. 2. Church work with youth—Case studies. 3. Cults—Controversial literature. 4. Christian sects—Controversial literature. 5. Pastoral theology—Case studies. I. Title.
    BV4446.M26   259   78-25976
    ISBN 0-8164-0436-4
    ISBN 0-8164-2211-7 (pbk.)

Second printing

1979 / *The Seabury Press*
815 Second Avenue / New York, N.Y. 10017

Printed in the United States of America
Designed by Victoria Gomez

Library of Congress Cataloging in Publication Data

Contents

The case histories presented in this book represent the actual experiences of the narrators as related to the author. In each instance, the names and circumstances have been altered in an attempt to protect the identities of those involved.

Whenever a group or religious leader is referred to in the case studies, pseudonyms have been chosen at random. Any pseudonym which suggests the actual name of any religious leader or group, living or in the past, should be recognized as a pseudonym. Such coincidences are inadvertent and I have tried to avoid them.

Introduction

It wasn't long ago that a discussion of "religious cults" would evoke a moderate response from a few listeners and polite boredom from most others. Although the anguish, which tore apart some families, occasionally made the headlines—PARENTS KIDNAP CHILD FROM RELIGIOUS LEADER, PARENTS SUED FOR $1 MILLION BY "RESCUED CHILD"—most Americans were rather apathetic.

Then in one grim twenty-four hour period in November 1978, life changed, not only for most members of new religious groups but also for most of America. The initial shock was bad enough: United States Congressman Leo Ryan, a hard-working factfinder from California, three highly-respected representatives of the news media, and one member of a group most people had never heard of were slain in a gruesome ambush at a jungle airport in South America. Their murderers were fellow Americans, members of the People's Temple. Their leader, Jim Jones, had started his group in San Francisco and had attracted national attention for his ability to draw together people of radically different backgrounds.

I remember the shock and outrage I felt that Sunday morning the news came in. And I recall, all too well, the total

1

hollowness I experienced when the death count started to reach the nine hundred mark. It was like a new report from the Vietnam War—nameless individuals slain in an unspeakable carnage, with their memories etched, for most of us, in the "official body count."

But those people were not slain by some vicious enemy bent on destroying another country. No, this body count was one of civilization's largest mass suicides, led by Jim Jones himself.

Before November 1978 and the massacre at Jonestown, Guyana, people would ask what might prompt such drastic reactions from parents that they would attempt to kidnap their own children. Why, in turn, would children turn against parents in such drastic legal actions? Is there a sense of overkill present? Or should we believe a few government officials and lawyers who assure us that Jonestown is an "isolated phenomenon"?

Or is its isolation limited to geography only? Are we safe to allow many groups whose leadership, structures, indoctrinations, and goals closely parallel, if not duplicate, the People's Temple to exist under the total protection of freedom of religion? Can a parent be glad that his child is interested in religion seriously enough to have sought out a "church" which meets his needs? And furthermore, isn't it commonly accepted in America that "all religion is good"? Could it be possible, in the light of Jonestown, that such a statement actually reflects a benign attitude toward religion which is seriously flawed?

Is it possible that the worst kind of evil can be disguised as religion?

Should the "established" congregations of the Christian and Jewish traditions, which historically have pervaded the moral foundations of this country, be concerned about the new religions? Is it, as many assert, the obligation of the historic, traditional Christian denominations to stand firm for the freedom of religion in this land and to encourage new expressions of religion? Should Christian and Jewish houses of worship open their doors to new religious groups?

Not long ago in New York, leaders of one of the largest "new religion" groups approached several pastors of local mainline denominational congregations, asking permission for the use of church facilities to hold "informal Bible studies."[1] But this same group, which described itself as "informal" to these pastors was actually the highly organized local expression of a "ministry" with thousands of followers around the English-speaking world, whose leader is considered by some followers as "the only person since the time of St. Paul who is able to interpret the scriptures correctly."[2] Such apparently deceptive approaches directed towards America's traditional religious establishment are not uncommon with a number of groups. Nor is such action limited to the United States. In the summer of 1978, one major group solicited funds in England while representing itself as co-workers with the Anglican (Episcopal) Church of England. Should we condone these actions?

What about the groups that use deceptive marketing techniques to gain new members? Some groups endeavor to hide the religious nature of the organization and the common spiritual bonds of the membership until new recruits have already established close relationships with the group and its individual members.

What about the present-day guru who claims to teach techniques of meditation that are represented to the public in the group's advertising as nonreligious? Can we accept the latter-day description of his techniques as nonreligious when his earlier writings clearly indicate the spiritual nature of the technique he is selling?[3] Do God-loving believers of both Jewish and Christian traditions have an obligation to respond to religious practices, however obscure or covert, that are in effect violations of the Ten Commandments?

But the questions cannot be directed only toward the new religions. How will the traditional religions respond when those people who question the validity of new-age religions turn against the historical denominations, condemning traditions and practices that are alien or threatening to them? In 1977, a young man who had converted to the Episcopal Church from a Baptist background was allegedly "deprogrammed" from an Episcopal congregation in Texas through the sponsorship of his concerned mother.[4] Some parents have reached the extreme of having offspring "deprogrammed" simply because the children have left their accustomed religious background to lead lives unfettered by any visible religious expressions. A few parents have felt that drastic action must be taken toward their children simply because a son or daughter has made a choice of marriage partner that the parents cannot understand or accept. Is "deprogramming" becoming a psychological game, in which Catholic parents can hire someone to draw their children away from Protestant heresy? Or would Christian parents steal their children away from a conversion to Judaism?

These are just a few of the questions that arise whenever people, concerned about the guarantee of religious freedom under the First Amendment to the United States Constitution, consider the questions surrounding religious cults.

Significant numbers of young adults, often from nominally religious backgrounds, have been drawn to expressions of religion that bear little resemblance to the mainstream of Christianity or Judaism. Within the past twenty years there has been a dawning of numerous "new" groups and movements, which span the scope of Christian understanding, and occasionally also Jewish thought, from ultraconservative orthodoxy to outright heresy. Some new religious groups do not even pretend to represent a "new facet" of western religious traditions; these groups have looked toward the wealth of eastern religious traditions for their point of reference, and often the departure for their own, occasionally unique, forms of heresy.

In 1975, the Episcopal bishop of Albany, N.Y., asked me to prepare some materials to help him respond to questions from parents who were concerned about their children's involvement in new religious goups. What started as a simple research project, which concerned itself with a variety of theological expressons, soon developed into a deep exploration of sociological, psychological, legal, and pastoral questions as well. For some, the question has been "How did we as parents go wrong?"; for others, "Shouldn't the cults be protected by the First Amendment's provisions for freedom of religion?" More than once, the ultimate question for many has been "What is best for the cult member?"—where the concept of "best" is limited to subjective concepts of success or failure that parents and clergy subscribe to. The questions themselves are endless.

I am *totally* committed to the concept of freedom of religion that the United States Constitution provides. However, I join those in the legal community who feel that such freedom is available only when preceded by both freedom of thought and freedom of association. Some cults deny these freedoms to their followers without prior warning that these basic freedoms will be withdrawn. I have met too many people who have "escaped from the cult scene" to be able to disallow totally the charges of "brainwashing" as "the emotional rants of disturbed parents," as one prominent religious leader labeled these charges.

Some may be disappointed that this book does not "name names" and make specific accusations against certain groups and leaders. There are several reasons for this basic decision to remain as general and as objective as possible within the main text. First of all, the bibliography lists a number of recent publications, some of superior quality, that offer both information and analysis of specific groups that have caused some degree of concern among clergy and families. I have attempted to offer some of the responses of these groups to their critics as well. I see little reason to duplicate such research in this book. Second, these new religious groups enjoy their own sort of process theology, often changing both teachings and methodology; anything that is too specific runs the danger of becoming outdated at a young age! Third, to limit a study to major groups that already receive a high level of public recognition is to ignore the equally valid concerns that hundreds of low-visibility new religions should prompt, although their spheres of influence are limited by numbers and geography. Finally, the first response of many new religions to any sort of scrutiny is usually to consider it as persecution from the opposition, designed to deprive believers of constitutional rights; such protestations from cult spokesmen often serve only to reinforce their influence on individual members.

Another consideration in the writing of this book was the use of the word "cult" to apply to certain religious groups that appear, in many instances, to be by-products of the post-Vietnam Zeitgeist, the "spirit of the times." For some people, any new religious group, or even an older group that has deviated from normal behavior, would be classified as a "cult"; however, these new religious groups, without exception, do not regard themselves as "cultic."

The concept of cult is not necessarily depreciatory in its general application. When we talk about a cult, we mean, first of all, a religious group that bears some significant difference, in one or more ways, of belief or practice from the groups that we would consider normative to our society.[5] By this definition, Christianity itself would have to be considered a cult by the people living around Jerusalem at the day of Pentecost and in the years immediately following; Christianity was new, radically different, unsettling to many observers. In a similar manner, the uproar in England during the mid-fifteen hundreds over the separation of the Catholic Church in England from the authority of the Bishop of Rome, to become the Church of England, would have prompted religious wags of that era to consider the newly emerging Anglicanism as a cult, and perhaps even a vicious one! Even today, great numbers of people are finding a new depth to their Christian pilgrimage through the phenomenon commonly called charismatic renewal or neopentecostalism; some observers of this religious awakening refer to it as "the cult of the paraclete."

However, our concern here about cultic religion is different. We want to consider those groups that abound today in many different forms, often appearing overnight and disappearing almost as quickly. The majority of these groups expound gnostic heresies[6]; some, furthermore, are alleged to employ classical brainwashing techniques to bring about their allegedly unholy conversions, while tearing apart the lives of many families.

These new cults share another characteristic: each group has its own living leader who professes either a messianic personality or a unique, divinely inspired interpretation of religious writings, usually the Bible. Many of these leaders have become quite wealthy as they have built up their religious empires by offering systems of spiritual growth or group involvement, which require the convert continually to be giving to the group either all or a significant portion of his income. Such groups demand obedience without questioning, see the world as filled with the devil, and subvert the basic teachings of both Christianity and Judaism.

The examples of allegedly harmful, deceptive, or criminal activities of the cults that are used in this book were chosen not because they are dramatic, although they occasionally are. Each example was chosen because it is representative of more than one major group; illustrations used are more often typical than extraordinary. While this allows for general observations to be drawn that may cut across the peculiarities of certain groups, such observations are in no way meant to imply that all cult groups share in the particular trait discussed. Whenever such universal application is appropriate, this fact will be made clear in the text.

We are on the verge of a radical upswing in the activities of such cults in the next decade; however, the spiritual ancestors of most such groups have been with us for centuries, in one form or another. Hopefully, this work will help you to understand the events that often drive people to rash actions about religious questions and issues, as well as the psychological changes that cult members often evince, the legal maze that must be followed, the radical alterations of family life that occasionally occur, some of the cultural factors that have allowed this question of cults to become so serious, and the responses that both parents and the more traditional religious groups can make.

In the past, religious observers have stated that such new spiritual groups would die out. Such claims were made in the mid-eighteen hundreds about a group with over four million members in 1978, almost twice as large as the Episcopal Church in the United States! History has shown that successful financial management and a willing public ensure that such groups not only can survive through the years but also flourish. Each observer, whether theologically trained or not, whether psychologically articulate or not, whether parent or child, must be able to make an informed appraisal of the cult phenomenon of the nineteen seventies.

In the four years I have worked with people involved in the questions surrounding the cults, I have met a great variety of people on *both* sides of the issues. Some cult spokesmen have been both patient and cordial toward me, while others have been defensive or outrightly hostile. In the same manner, the parents and clergy I have encountered range from reasonable, thinking, and caring people to some whose frustrations and anger have grown into consuming hatred and suspicion; happily, the former example is much more typical of the people I have met.

There is no doubt that some people are extremely sensitive to anything that appears contrary to their personal feelings about new religious groups. It is not uncommon for cults to construct legal problems for those who would criticize them. A few parents and family members of cult followers have acted in a totally unfitting manner, including outright falsification of identity to gain the information they desire.

When fear and suspicion become the dominant emotions of a person, the actions that emerge are often extreme. I had an opportunity in mid-nineteen seventy-eight to speak to a gathering of concerned individuals in Los Angeles, and I took along the youth minister of my parish so he would have an opportunity to hear the parents' version of what their children had encountered "in the name of God." While our youth director was engaged in a conversation with a parent, the brother of a cult member came up behind him, seized him, and attempted to yank his wig off, thereby disclosing the identity of a cult member who had infiltrated the meeting. There was a problem, though. My youth minister was not a member of a cult, nor was he wearing a wig to cover a distinctively shaved head. Paranoia on the part of family members? Yes. But that same man had taken a similar action at an earlier conference and discovered the distinctive bald head and pony tail of a new religion under that wig! It was apparent that one group was concerned enough about the meeting of a few involved parents that they would resort to subterfuge in order to infiltrate the meeting.

My own experiences while writing this book have convinced me that some persons or groups have been intensely concerned about what I would say. I have had personal conversations with spokesmen for several new religions, who were concerned about what *Carnival of Souls* would say; in one instance, the spokesman went so far as to suggest that I had "better let our people review what you have said before it is published."

However, the real challenge has been found in the subtle, and not so subtle, threats mailed to me, my ecclesiastical superiors, and even members of my parish; in fact, people have emerged from church services to find their cars covered with inflammatory material directed toward me simply because I would ask questions about another religion. In one letter, a person claimed to be upset about my "cult sermons," even though I had not preached any! In another letter, typed on the same day and apparently on the same typewriter, a "law student at a California University" (sic) sent a letter, purportedly addressed to cult leaders, suggesting a number of legal avenues they might pursue against me. Of course, the obligatory copies of this were sent to both my ecclesiastical superiors and my publisher.

Four days later, another "fact sheet" about me came through the mail and was then distributed surreptitiously on our church's parking lot through the apparent sponsorship of the "Subcommittee to Investigate Parental Abuse" of "Americans United to Protect Constitutional Rights." One person expressed his distress that no address or phone number was given for the group; they could not join it, even if they agreed with what was said!

The statements made are absurd at the least. My "controversial stance [against the cults] alienated [MacCollam] from his bishop and he was forced to flee to the West Coast." Nothing was said about the support, occasionally both practical and spiritual, that my bishop constantly offered me in this reasearch, nor the favorable response he had to earlier works such as "The Weekend that Never Ends." "Fleeing to the West Coast" reminds me of the preacher who was run out of town on a rail, only to get a much better position in his next parish. Rather than being run out of town to "flee to the

West Coast," my move was carefully considered and represented a most happy personal and professional change! Other allegations about the receipt of money from "deprogramming sources" to enable me to buy an "expensive home" overlook the minor factors of a supportive and generous parish vestry as well as my family. Of course, my banker played no small role in buying a home!

It would be a gross understatement to claim that a few people have been mildly curious about what *Carnival of Souls* is all about!

Literally hundreds of people offered assistance to me in the gathering of material for this book. Because some interview subjects are themselves enmeshed in the legal tangle surrounding cults or have family members still in cults, I have elected to single out no particular individuals for recognition. The people whose stories are told will, I trust, be glad that their experiences may give some glimmer of hope or wisdom to others in the future. For those whose stories could not be shared here, I trust that they will realize that omissions were prompted solely by the need to economize on space.

I am grateful to the people to whom I have ministered while this book matured, both in Schuylerville, N.Y., and Glendale, California. If Wilbur Hogg, bishop of Albany, had not instilled me with both vision and courage, this book might not have happened. Most of all, I am indebted to my family. They have inspired me to attempt to insure that my own children will grow up in a country where they have the freedom insured to them that their choices of religious belief will emerge from the functioning of their own free wills, free of deception and free of coercion.

Joel A. MacCollam
Glendale, California
1 January 1979

chapter 1

New Religions

When Galt McDermott wrote the rock musical *Hair* in the late 1960s, the most popular song to emerge was "The Age of Aquarius." Those years were the dawning of a new era for the religious establishment in America; social prophets such as Ronald Enroth foretold the rise of cults, as well as other forms of new religious groups, as early as the dawning of the first lights of the Aquarian age, in such books as *The Jesus Generation*.[1] Many people in mainline Christian churches were beginning to discover a deeper commitment and expression of their Christian faith through pentecostal experiences or being "born again"; even such conservative groups as the Episcopal and Roman Catholic traditions have discovered thousands of their members who have been "born again" and express strong desires to "spread the Good News" throughout the world. The late 1960s saw not only the emergence of several cult groups but also the public manifestations of the "Jesus movement," a return to biblical life-styles, deeper appreciation for scriptural teachings, and the beginnings of some of the "superchurches" around the land.

But there was another stream of activity in America's religious life that would prove to be not as readily welcomed as the "Jesus movement" or neopentecostalism. "New" religious groups drew the attention of many people, groups that promulgated strange-sounding theologies, radical changes in life-style, deep commitment, and promises of a "better world." Strange groups of young people, decked out in yellow robes, heads shaven except for a tassel of hair that resembled a ponytail, were dancing on the sidewalks of New York's Greenwich Village the same night that *Hair* opened on Broadway. Their earnest faces and strong entreaties to passersby indicated a religious fervor that was both alien and uncomfortable to most who encountered them.

Walking in Manhattan that same evening, a person might have received an opportunity to view a free movie about a movement that claimed to present a means of self-discovery. On another corner the opportunity was offered to go off on a weekend retreat for "sharing and fellowship" under the sponsorship of a group that represented itself as a Christian church (and still does ten years later, in spite of overwhelming evidence, both theological and ethical, to the contrary).

Out of those humble beginnings on the streets of many American cities has arisen the first spiritual generation of the new "age of Aquarius," the new religions, which some observers, either out of convenience or distrust, call "cults." Their members walk down the street and wish you an earnest "God bless you"; cult members will often appear very "normal" in outward appearance and dress as well as in actions. This first generation of new religions is causing a great debate in many fields. Psychiatrists and psychologists argue whether members of cults are under some sort of harmful influence that brings about a personality change or "brainwashing." The legal profession is caught in a constitutional tangle involving "freedom of religion"; someday, the courts may have to determine whether certain groups actually do use the techniques of coercive persuasion that their critics allege. Sociologists wonder how American youth can be so attracted to religions that often are very obviously cultural transplants.

No one knows exactly how many cults exist today or how many people are committed to such groups; some estimates include as many as three million people involved in over a thousand groups. On the other hand, experts may be unduly optimistic in feeling that only a few thousand people are involved in new religious groups. Of course, the estimates will vary, in part because the groups that one "expert" might call a cult would not be considered dangerous or harmful by another observer. If you look at the world from the viewpoint of conservative protestantism, the absence of scriptural orthodoxy might be enough to label a particular group as a cult, regardless of the psychological or legal questions that the group might (or might not) pose. Many expressions of neo-pentecostalism are considered "cultic" by traditional Christians simply because the rituals involved are different from more traditional expressions of worship. Would it be reasonable to label Buddhism a cult simply because a Jewish child converted to that religion? It is not enough to label a group as a "cult" and thereby infer that something sinister is happening within the group unless more pressing questions than style of worship, or perhaps even theological pureness, are raised.

The cults are here to stay, in one form or another. They are not decreasing in size, as some would like to imagine. One particular group was considered by many knowledgeable observers to be on the wane and not worth considering as a major force among new religions any more. But in early 1978 that same group was able to attract some six thousand followers to a national convention in a major American city. The secular press had no knowledge of the convention's existence until the adjournment! Even if a group's popularity (and therefore perhaps also its income) begins to fade, leaders are usually able to bring forth some new revelation or temptation for the public to ponder; the lure of new, more exciting levels of experience and knowledge keeps many followers interested in their spiritual masters and churches.

How shall we relate to these new religions? Are they legitimate expressions of the relationship between God and man which are passing through the awkward stages of early life, like a child who is learning to walk and falls on his face? Or are these groups, either individually or collectively, a sinister force bent on destroying the fabric of American society? People are raising these diametrically opposed claims about new religious groups, but what can we do with these claims? How can we arrive at some reasonable determination of a group's legitimacy as a religion, and, in turn, its right to constitutional protection as a religion?

Evaluating the New Religions

Many religions can point to persecutions that followers experienced in the early years of faith experience. Christians underwent extreme persecution at the hands of several Roman emperors, and were even thrown to the lions. Death by stoning was an all-too-real fate, which many Christians had to look forward to; in spite of this, Christianity flourished. Protestants were persecuted by Roman Catholics during the Spanish Inquisition. England was often a bloodbath in the wake of the founding of the Church of England and the ensuing tensions between Catholic (Roman) and Catholic (English) believers in the years before the reign of Elizabeth I.

The cults often refer to such experiences within the history of Christianity as analogous to their own; "we are new, and we are being persecuted because of our newness." The argument can be pursued in a manner quite favorable to the position of the cult: "Look at the Christians; they were persecuted because they were sent by God. And we also are persecuted because we have been sent by God." However, such analogies, perhaps interesting to ponder, do not provide enough information to determine the legitimacy of a group or any thread of solid relationship to Christian experience.

Religious persecution that is grounded solely on the

newness of a religion is evil—and also illegal. But many people in America hear of a group describing itself as "religious" and slip into a benign attitude toward the group. "If it is religious, it must be good" is the simple statement that too many people are quick to accept without any consideration of the implications of such an attitude. Do we have a right to question a group that presents itself as a religion? Should we raise questions about a "religious" group that shows itself strongly interested in monumental real estate, commercial ventures, and politics, perhaps at the expense of its religious work? What about a religious group that stresses the breakup of family life, that uses recruiting techniques that are fraught with deception? Not only do we have the right to question such practices performed in the name of religion, but we have the obligation to question the motivations of such groups, whether they are only just emerging in this post-Aquarian age or have existed in some form for thousands of years. Religion can be corrupt, and we need to establish some sort of guideline to direct our thinking toward a careful examination of all aspects of a religion's activities.

Any observer of the religious scene *must* remember the fact that a religion is different does not automatically infer that the religion is bad. Christianity at its inception was radically different, in both theology and life-style. How many people, aside from the bands of early Christians, lived together in totally committed community or were so zealous about the Messiah? Yes, early Christians (and some contemporary Christians) have shown their faith experiences to be radically different, but the test that Jesus Christ would apply to his followers and imitators is based on the fruits of the religion, not on the degree of difference: "By their fruits ye shall know them."[2]

Rather than automatically labeling a radically different group as "harmful," we must examine the problem from another perspective. Too many critics of new religious life-styles see traditional religion, and particularly most expressions of Christianity, as a means of improving a person's life "where it is at"; these observers feel that *anything* that leads a person to a radical new life-style or system of values must therefore be a harmful cult. However, even Christian tradition is filled with examples of people who have been called into different life-styles or whose lives were radically altered (at least by their own standards). What about Francis of Assisi or the other great and holy founders of the ancient monastic orders? We don't consider them cult leaders! These people who led others into changed life-styles were not changed by anything malicious, either deceptive or manipulative! An even more classic example of radical conversion would have to be the life of Saul of Tarsus, who encountered the risen Christ on the road to Damascus and underwent a powerful, and radical, conversion experience.[3] Saul was turned around from a zealous love of the law of Judaism to his role as perhaps the foremost early Apostle of Christianity; the radical change in his life can be examined by its fruits, as well as by its sources. Did Paul become a mindless robot, following the dictates of some leader who was getting rich off his hard labors? Did Paul become a person consumed by hate, rebelling against the authority structures of his time, or was he driven by love and willing to spend substantial periods in prison for his faith? Was his conversion an event carefully orchestrated by leaders of a weekend retreat or something genuinely authored for Paul's life by God himself?

Some new religious groups have earned the pejorative title of *cult* because of their own actions; if people ask questions about them, cult leaders need only look to their own groups and their individual members to discover the sources of the problems and to administer solutions. There are several questions that deserve to be considered about any religious group, and particularly the new religions, which many allege are harmful and therefore cults. These questions are especially applicable to groups that are either new or unfamiliar. There are few groups that would bear the burden of manifesting all of these traits. However, there are several major and numerous smaller groups, which conform in some detail to a majority of these traits and, in turn, are causing many questions to be asked about the legitimacy of cult religions.

TECHNIQUES OF CONVERSION

It is possible to enlist in a religious cult and not be aware that the group is in fact religious in nature, even after several weeks of involvement. Some groups deliberately operate under a veil of deception while recruiting, perhaps presenting themselves as a collection of concerned individuals who do social research or who seek to change the world. One recent newspaper advertisement in a large eastern city was sponsored by a well-known cult in the "Personals" section of the newspaper: "Wanted for unique street ministry. Young adults who love Jesus and want to help others. Call Greg at . . . for details."[4] While this ad sounds both innocent and well motivated, the group paying for it is Christian in name, but not in theology or methodology. It is this same group that recruits on the streets of certain American cities by distributing pamphlets which describe its social vision and alleged affiliations with traditional community agencies. In one notable example, the group's distribution claimed a connection with a hospital operated by the Salvation Army, although that organization did not even know of the existence of the cult's recruiting organization.[5]

Does the group in question bring about conversions through manipulative techniques? Does the inductee get a well-balanced diet that is sufficient for his nutritional needs? Does he get enough sleep? Is he allowed the comforts of adequate plumbing? Is there an opportunity for privacy, or is his person degraded to the point that his self-esteem risks collapse?

Conversions may be reinforced among the members of certain groups, not only by manipulative techniques and the allegations of persecution made by certain cult leaders but also by certain attributes of daily living, such as a group's strong emphasis on a team effort for successful fund raising or street recruiting. Members of one group stress radical street attire because it helps members feel as though they "belong to each other" in public, both for protection and for the feeling of being "socially secure." As long as members of this group were together, they felt strengthened in their common cause, "because we looked so weird."[6]

LEADERSHIP

All cults have a leader who is very powerful and attractive to his followers, and usually very much alive. Does the leader claim to be a Messiah figure? Is he revered by his followers as the only person who is able to give authoritative teachings from Scriptures? Does the leader function as a strong central authority without whose guidance the group or its individual members are unable to reach decisions, or even incapable of functioning? Is the leader acquiring either personal wealth or great personal comfort at the personal expense of lesser members?

A historical analogy can be made between certain cult leaders and their churches to the *episcopi vagantes*, the "wandering bishops" who were once recognized clergy in traditional Christian expressions (often Roman Catholic or Anglican) and who chose to establish their own peculiar churches, with themselves as the ecclesiastical overseers, the "bishops." Whether these men became bishops through legitimate means and then started their own flocks is not as important as whether or not these men exercised their apparent authority in a legitimate manner. In too many instances, the churches over which such "bishops" presided appear to exist, if they exist at all except on paper, for the sake of the bishops, rather than the church leaders existing for the sake of their churches. Some authorities report that such "wandering bishops" have existed without even the pretense of an organized church to either support them or to uphold their authority.[7] Could it be that some cults actually exist for little more than the ego needs or financial hunger of its leaders?

AUTHORITY

In many groups, the lists and rules are unending and often degrading. Methods for personal sanitary habits are even proscribed by several smaller groups. In one major group, it is a "sin" reportable to the authority figures for a person to sit down without permission; in this same group, "baby Christians" are constantly followed by "pastors," who monitor each movement and statement, reporting any deviations from the group's norms.[8] Does the group in question require blind obedience, totally unquestioning, to every command or whim that the authority figures put forth?

LEGAL NORMS

Does the group in question function willingly within the law, or does it attempt to sidestep its obligations to society? The basic question, which we will examine later, is whether or not the group guarantees the constitutional rights of its membership. In addition, though, other legal standards, including criminal and tax laws, should be examined. For example, some groups charge for the courses they offer; in some instances, this in itself might not be questionable. However, if a group charges for a course, does it call the money required a "donation" or "tuition"? Only one (the tuition) is legal, because the money paid to the group is for the benefit of the person taking the course.[9]

In the state of New York, one major group was barred by

the attorney general from mail solicitations within that state because of alleged fraudulent use of funds solicited through the mails from New York residents. The cult sent forth appeals for groups with ostensible academic, religious, or cultural goals that might benefit the communities solicited. However, the New York investigation showed that a disproportionately small amount of the funds raised was actually designated by the parent organization (unnamed in the fund appeals) for the solicited purposes. The remainder went to the parent organization for its own discretionary use, without regard to the merits of that use in the eyes of the donors.

Another group strongly criticized by the attorney general of New York withdrew most of its members to Europe three years ago, where their press coverage and public image were more favorable; this same group has retained its customary methods and ideals, while recently changing the name of the group and also the name (but not the person) of the leader as it seeks now to reestablish itself in the United States. This group instructed its members to commit criminal acts to meet their daily needs for food. Because members were special to God, they were encouraged by their prophetic leader to steal in order to support the group. If they did not have enough money to purchase food for the local commune, the members would go to the nearest grocery store and steal what they needed, because they were so special to God. They actually believed that this was a God-given right bestowed uniquely on them![10] Another group has advised its membership to use all "heavenly deceptions" available to raise money for the group or to further its cause in any other manner (including recruitment).[11]

Groups that arise out of other cultures and bring their members to the United States have often run afoul of the Immigration and Naturalization Service. Some six hundred immigrants, members of one organization, were ordered deported in April 1977 because their alleged purpose for residence in the United States, "religious education and training," was being fulfilled primarily through the solicitation of funds and the selling of merchandise on the streets.[12]

FINANCIAL PROCEDURES

The most obvious feature of many new religious groups is the wealth that surrounds the principal leaders, particularly the group's chief leader, whether Messiah figure or prophet. While this wealth usually is not controlled directly by the leader, such instances do occur; most new groups have some form of corporate board that exerts at least the appearance of control over financial matters. However, it is apparent that some leaders enjoy a standard of living, and indeed a standard of luxury and convenience, that is well beyond the grasp of the rank and file. Whether these leaders are able to divert corporate funds to their personal use through legitimate means or otherwise is a question open to speculation, because most of these new religious groups are totally secretive about their financial structures (as is their legal right at this point in time). Several leaders of new religions reside in plush mansions, which are fully staffed either at the religion's expense or with members of the group, while the leaders fly around the country in private jets and enjoy fleets of luxury surface vehicles while earthbound. Some cults are little more than the same sort of "pyramid" financial structure that has been used successfully in many businesses; those who buy into the plan early in its existence may reap vast benefits, while those who get involved later on have a decreasing chance of financial success.

The means of gathering financial resources are as multitudinous as the infinite variety of groups involved; one group considers legal proceedings against critics as a viable means of fund raising! The same group investigated by the attorney general of New York, whose members fled to Europe, also drew marked criticism for its retention of members' property. "No ex-member was permitted to retain any of the possessions he 'contributed' nor to take them out when he left. In view of the brainwashing techniques . . . there is a real question as to whether members are exercising their free will when they 'donate' their possessions . . ."[13]

One measure of the fruits of a group is its level of charitable work, particularly with its material and financial resources. Some cults have made widely publicized claims of helping the poor, and indeed they do. But while the claims are true, the aid given to the poor is often slight when held in comparison to either the net worth of the organization or its annual income. One group claimed to give twenty-two thousand pounds of fresh fruit to poor people in southern California in 1976; while this gift was actually made (and highly publicized), the total amount given represents only a very small portion of the group's annual agricultural productivity and other food interests.

It is not unreasonable to look at the investments of a group to see whether the leaders are investing in people, perhaps through the development of programs to help those needing help, or in making more money. Several tax-free religious corporations manage large commercial operations, including farms, fishing operations, publishing houses, secular newspapers, major real estate holdings in metropolitan centers, and even retail stores. One group recently purchased a large onion farm in upstate New York; the same group is making extensive investments in the commercial fishing industry along the Atlantic seaboard. In both instances, considerable local concern has been voiced that this particular group will be able to manage its commercial operations at a high level of profit, and even at unfairly competitive prices, because the group has a large and cheap labor force to draw upon in its membership.

Still another group has advertised to its membership the opportunity to help further its cause by investing funds, which they might not be able to donate in long-term notes held by the organization and paying 6 percent interest. Claiming to be "backed by God," the group offers its members an unusual way of furthering their religious dollars.[14]

But we still have not exhausted the great variety of financial maneuvers that some groups employ. One group is particularly known for its aggressive solicitations in public places, especially airports; they will approach likely contacts with the offer of a magazine or record and then demand a donation once the proffered merchandise is accepted. This same group sends its membership out on the streets dressed in Santa Claus suits around the Christmas holidays, setting up their membership in competition with traditional groups such as the Salvation Army through the use of those groups' long-established and carefully maintained public identities. This technique of fund raising proved so effective in one major city that the cult Santas were required to wear white belts, while the more traditional Santas continued to wear their accustomed black belts. This was the only means available to the public for distinguishing the traditional Santas from the cult members!

Perhaps the ultimate fraud in gathering financial resources is perpetuated by a cult that is well known in the southwest United States and had its legitimate beginnings in the early days of the Jesus Movement. The group's resource is huge: the welfare budgets of many governments that have been paying the medical bills of cult members. A former member writes that "the irony of it all shows up when the leader, on her television show, tells the audience how the 'Lord blesses' the group with new properties, cars, expensive apartments, furniture, etc. The impression of wealth does not coincide with state-aid payments." [15]

Americans are particularly willing to give to something that is represented as either charitable or religious, without asking questions about the ultimate aims of a group. When I lived in upstate New York in a town of just over twelve hundred individuals, one cult visited my door several times within the course of one year. Even though the town's clergy had issued a public statement in the local newspaper warning the citizens of deceptive fund raising, the group continued to return, probably because their efforts at fund raising were proving to be successful. The most common ruse was to solicit funds for a "new Bible school downstate." This appeal was guaranteed to appeal to basically conservative, Church-oriented people in a small American town; the fund raisers would admit only with great reluctance that they represented a religion that, in fact, rejected most of the Bible in favor of its own unique scripture, authored allegedly by their Messiah leader. While the Bible was taught at their new seminary, the clearly prominent scriptural work studied was their own original scripture.

SOCIOLOGICAL PROBLEMS

Many parents allege that relationships with their children, which they considered "close," have been shattered by cult groups. Former cult members claim that the cults branded anyone outside of the group or opposed to it as "possessed of Satan," tools of the devil to be avoided at all costs ("And a man's foes shall be they of his own household").[16] Even if this particular wedge is not driven between members and their families, regular communication may be difficult to maintain because the followers move about the country on short notice, whenever the group requires their presence in another community.

Some groups appear to rob people of their life's direction, turning members' attention toward God and the group, while also encouraging them to abandon their formal education in favor of what the cult offers. On the other hand, there are groups that do exactly the opposite; they do not encourage people to leave their educational pursuits or secular jobs and professions for the sake of the group. These groups either recognize the benefits that the group will enjoy from members who can utilize a practical skill or feel that members "make a better witness" when they live in the community. Groups that do assume the responsibility for educating their members bear an awesome accountability for insuring that members are able to use their minds logically and in a manner that allows them to function normally in society. The danger is present that some groups have already produced members who are able to function only within the authority and support structures of the group; stripped of that buttress, they are unable to make even the simple decisions of everyday life. One cult member who was ejected from the group and chose to rejoin her parents required over two hours simply to choose several new pairs of socks at a discount store;[17] while this is perhaps an extreme example, it does represent the sort of mental trauma that can arise out of a cult experience.

Some groups have gone so far as to require that marriage partners be either selected or approved by the group's leadership. In fact, it is alleged to be possible in one group to have your partner preselected and then to be "married" without any of the customary legal sanctions; the relationship is recognized by the group, but it lacks either the permission of the state to marry as granted through a license, or the witness of a representative of the state.[18]

Another group is alleged to strip converts not only of material goods but also marriage mates. A former member reports that she "donated" her car "for the Lord's use" and discarded much of her clothing, which was not acceptable to the group's dress standards. She then continues on the sacrifices of marital relationships that couples were forced to observe: "Even married couples joining the group would be separated during the first three months. The wife would live with the

single 'sisters' and the husband with the unmarried 'brothers.' . . . The couple could be together only during chap-
eroned congregational gatherings. [The leader] even caused
couples to separate or divorce when a husband or wife would
leave. The remaining spouse was told to forsake the 'back-
slided' mate and continue to serve the Lord." [19]

There are blatant attempts in some groups to assign
women to tasks that may work both to lower their sociological
status and to induce psychological trauma. In one major
group, women are relegated to maintaining the worship facilities and living quarters of the group; no greater responsibility is allowed. In another group, women are encouraged to
go out as "flirty fish" and to thereby offer themselves as free
prostitutes in an effort to produce converts; the most attractive women in the group offer their bodies in the hopes of
"witnessing" about God through sexual acts. In yet another
group, women desiring to have "perfect babies" are required
to have sexual relationships not only with their husbands but
also with one preselected male member from each of the
other eleven signs of the zodiac.

PSYCHOLOGICAL TRAUMAS

Closely aligned with the sociological problems are the psychological upsets that some people allege the cults perpetrate
on their members. "Group think" is a very present danger in
such organizations, as well as many other facets of society.
Accusations are made by parents and former members that
techniques of persuasion are used that effectively block out
the member's past in an apparently successful effort at
"brainwashing" or hypnosis. Most of the questioned groups
deny that they use coercive techniques without the permission of the inductee, justifying these apparent excesses or
abuses as part of the fervor of the organization.

POLITICAL DANGERS

Cults, like most religious organizations, do attempt to influence the political and legislative life of America through efforts at lobbying. Whether it is wrong for religious groups to represent their concerns and viewpoints to lawmakers is a delicate question that is beyond the scope of this book. However, we must remain fair and apply the same standards when we consider the lobbying efforts of traditional religious-interest groups. We must insist that all groups exerting influence in the political realm are doing so in full compliance with the legal standards set for such activity.

How can we view the religious nature of a particular group if, as some allege, the group and its leadership represent the interests of a foreign government? What about a group that puts forth followers as candidates for public office? One group has already done so, and another is considering such a move, in the hope of a more sympathetic ear in the national legislature. Some citizens have cried "foul" because these new religious groups are able to move substantial numbers of followers into an area, either to promote "block voting" or to saturate the area with campaign workers.

At least one major group has aspirations of leading the United States into a new era. Commenting on the tensions between North Korea and South Korea, one popular cult leader reflected on his own political plans as early as 1973:

> I have a master strategy to win America, and they [the leaders] did not know or truly understand my entire strategy. Therefore, when I as Commander-in-Chief landed in America, there should have been troops to join and engage in the greatest battle ever. But that order was not there. So, in the entire year of 1972, instead of engaging in the outward battle, I had to reestablish our own ranks myself.[20]

This same religious leader sees members of his group as the future political leadership of America:

> If the U.S. continues its corruption, and we find among the senators and congressmen no one really usable for our purposes, we can make senators and congressmen out of our members. . . . I have met many famous—so-called "famous"—senators and congressmen, but to my eyes they are just nothing; they are weak and helpless before God. They are scared to think it might be possible that they will not be re-elected. . . . But I am not going to send you into the political field right away—but later on when we are prepared.[21]

EXCLUSIVE THOUGHT SYSTEMS

Some groups live in such isolation from society that their members have no contact with information from the outside world; newspapers, radios, and television are forbidden. Other groups discourage their followers from reading such "outside influences" because of the works of the devil outside the group. Does a group in question allow members to read only one translation of Scripture (usually the Authorized Version of 1611), while recommending that only the teachings approved by the group be read, or is there freedom to pursue other resources and to voice contrary opinion?

THEOLOGY

Does the group in question actually represent what it claims to be? Can a group call itself "Christian" and be considered a viable member of the Christian community when it denies almost every major doctrinal foundation that the rest of Christianity has held as essential for over fifteen hundred years? Can we hold as legitimate the theology of a group that sets the Bible as its absolute, first and final source for revelation and direction, and then selectively reads most of the Scriptures to pass over those sections that do not agree easily with the stated opinions and directions of the leadership? How is it that such a group can set its own standards for theological purity and then turn around and almost immediately violate their own standards? [22]

Some groups are seeking to change the face of the earth by establishing either a foothold or a congenial relationship with established religions. The cult leader who says of himself that "out of all the saints sent by God, I think I am the most successful one" feels that subterfuge is essential to establishing his theological perspective and position. "In order for us to be able to *manipulate* [emphasis added] all the denominations of the world, we must first of all be able to influence theological scholars." [23] The theology of this "Christian" group was carefully studied by the National Council of Churches, and their application for membership was turned down, in large part because the theology presented in their scriptures offers a total rejection of biblical Christianity, in spite of the public protestations to the contrary of the group's leadership.

This same group claims that its leader is not the Messiah; but former members report asking this question about the leader and receiving a very pointed answer. They were led solemnly into a room that was adorned only with a picture of the group's leader and allowed to stand in silence. Even a casual examination of the official publications of the group suggests that the leader is accorded a messianic status:

> Few were aware of the universal significance of the quiet Bethlehem scene 2,000 years ago when Jesus Christ, Son of God, was born. The saying "history is made at night" was again proven in 1920. On January 6 of that year an event of similar significance took place. . . . On this day, unnoticed by all, a child was born who was destined to be appointed the most difficult task in history—remaking the world. History will mark this day as the beginning of a cosmic transition. [24]

How can we respect the rights of a religious group that engages in deliberately false advertising by denying the religious roots of its tradition? Such a group has been offering techniques for relaxation clearly announced as nonreligious, in spite of the early writings of the group's leader concerning meditation as the path to God. In fact, the religious nature of this organization has been sufficiently documented that the group is no longer allowed to present its teachings and techniques in the public schools of New Jersey, just one of the states where the techniques have been offered, often through the support of funds solicited from governmental agencies, including the United States Army War College and several prison boards.[25]

THE USE OF DECEPTION

This last example of misleading advertising is a prime example of the types of deception that some groups use. A legitimate religion will make mistakes, in part because every religion is made up of fallible human beings; such mistakes can be forgiven. But can we so easily overlook or forgive the faults of groups that deliberately and continually encourage members to steal or to use "heavenly deception" to accomplish their ends? Does not a God-centered religion have some obligation to convey to its followers a system of morality that respects the rights of other human beings and encourages honesty? Or is a religion to be allowed to make whatever claims of a nontheological nature it desires that would further its cause, with absolutely no regard to the truth of such nontheological assertions? The distinction is offered here between theological and nontheological assertions because for many people the theological conceptions they hold about God are highly subjective and difficult to evaluate without some commonly held standard of reference. However, I find it difficult to remain as generous when such conditions are to be applied to basic matters involving human integrity and outrightly deceptive practices that are encouraged by the leadership of certain groups.

ANTI-SEMITISM

One of the traditional faith groups very concerned about cults is the Jewish community; Jewish leaders are keenly sensitive about the aggressive attitudes that certain groups display toward their traditions and their people. While this concern embraces the missionary efforts of certain Christian evangelical groups directed specifically toward the Jewish community, it focuses primarily on the outright hatred that some groups have expressed toward Jews. A further concern of Jewish leadership is that eventually there may be no more Jews because of their assimilation into other religions and cultures.

SELLING SALVATION AND GOD

Some groups offer their systems for salvation or finding God only for a price; they base this practice on the need to engender commitment from the people taking their courses. Cults counter charges about these practices with the rationale that even traditional theological colleges must charge tuition and that church groups charge registration fees for weekend conferences. While some charges may indeed be levied by traditional groups to cover expenses of the event or to maintain a school for advanced study, the basic message of salvation is given without cost. You can listen to a sermon and not have to donate; you can take a Bible-study course in most churches and not have to pay a tuition, although a person might have to purchase materials for the course. But there is no profit motive!

Christians and Jews can recall together the wisdom of the prophet Isaiah: "Ho, everyone that thirsteth, come ye to the waters, and he that hath no money, come ye, buy and eat; yea, come buy wine and milk without money, and without price."[26] The Christian community can reach further into its biblical traditions and ponder the words of the Apostle Paul: "And not as it was by one that sinned, so is the gift: for the judgment was by one to condemnation, but the *free gift* [emphasis added] is of many offenses unto justification."[27] Any group that requires a financial commitment that suggests "purchasing" a walk with God deserves close scrutiny.

In conclusion, just as you can tell a leopard by its stripes, so, too, you can recognize a cult quite often by its fruits. In evaluating a religious experience that is different to us, the above traits may prove to be an initial guideline. However, the fact that a particular group seems to fit most or all of these categories does not automatically make a group evil. The key word is *seems;* many people have become quick to judge and label new religious groups as pernicious cults only because the group is different or because of the rumors they have heard. Before accusing any group of manipulating its members or deceptive practices, some sort of concrete documentation is needed. Without this documentation, people looking at this religious phenomenon run the risk of becoming little more than vigilante groups. On the other hand, the new religions that are legitimate should have nothing to hide or to fear from careful scrutiny.

chapter 2

Profiles of Recruits

The cult experience appeals to a wide variety of people, both young and old. Of course, the overwhelming majority of cult inductees are between the ages of eighteen and thirty; however, some groups number on their rolls the parents and even the grandparents of younger members. Nor is the cult experience directed toward any particular ethnic or economic group, although there appears to be a disproportionately high number of college-educated, white, middle-class young people involved. This perhaps reflects the socioeconomic profiles of the student bodies at most colleges where cults recruit rather than a desire on the part of the cults to be exclusivistic in seeking members.

Spiritual Counterfeits Project in Berkeley, California, has made extensive contact with both cult members and former cult members in their effort to relate accurately both the theologies of these new religions and also the Christian theological response. These researchers see the most susceptible potential converts as idealists and intellectuals who are drawn to philosophical and theological systems of thought, which include absolutes on the meaning of life and incentives for changing the world. People who have recently experienced a conversion experience to Christianity but have established no roots in the traditional Christian community have also been shown to be ready targets for recruiting that represents the cult as Christian. Of course, the lonely and the alienated are vulnerable, as well as those people who desire a different quality of intimacy in their lives.[1]

While many aspects of the overall answer to the basic question of "Who is attracted?" run parallel to some aspects of the recruiting methodologies of cults, it may be helpful to restate these characteristics from the perspective of the potential convert rather than from the cult's viewpoint.

CULTS APPEAL TO YOUNG ADULTS

Men and women in the eighteen to twenty-five age bracket are most vulnerable to the appeal of the cults, but individuals from other age groups are by no means exempt; I have interviewed parents who joined groups and then induced their children to follow in their footsteps. Cults are usually hesitant to recruit children under age eighteen because of the legal ramifications. However, cults are eager to welcome people from the older age groups who find some personal need fulfilled by the cult or its individual members or who simply give moral or financial support to the cult's work because "it sounds so nice, and they do such good things."

Psychiatrists have described many young adults in cults as self-identified failures who come from families of overachievers. Recent studies suggest that upwards of 58 percent of cult inductees may have suffered from some sort of personality disorder before they entered the cult; these same studies suggest that the personality disorders noted may have led to a predisposition towards joining such a regimented group offering either escapism or absolute values for life.[2] Borderline schizophrenia is perhaps the most commonly indicated problem. However, it is significant to note that the remaining 42 percent of cult members surveyed manifested no indications of prior emotional problems. In fact, many cult members have been described by parents and friends, as well as clergy and doctors, as totally normal individuals before their association with their new-found religious group.

One parent who lost a child for six years to a cult talks of the six "I's" that are the personality traits of potential recruits: innocence, idealism, inquisitiveness, independence, identity crisis, and insecurity.[3] As one example, we can take the story of Sharon, a young woman in the vulnerable age group of eighteen to thirty, who joined an ultrafundamentalistic Christian group in the southwest United States at a crisis time in her life, even though she was already a committed Christian. Part of her problem rested in her lack of a church in which to express her faith commitment; another part of her problem was reflected in the difficult transition she was going through in her personal and professional life:

> . . . my difficulties at work in managing the incorrigible kids; at school with finances; and my dissatisfaction over not being able to find a professional job and a church, contributed to my decision to forsake all. Also, I was in the process of filling out applications to several missions boards for service. Because of these factors, during the first week with the group I was at a vulnerable point of noncommittal, indecision, insecurity, dissatisfaction, and disappointment. Thus, the alternative offered at the Group seemingly fulfilled my desire to serve God and my need for total commitment. And in making the decision, the other depressive factors were replaced by new plans, new life style, and a new environment. The Group interpreted the whole situation for me as the Lord stripping me down to the point of repentance to serve Him.[4]

PEOPLE WHO SEEK A SENSE OF FULFILLMENT

Many people are growing to feel that our technological-materialistic society has created a spiritual vacuum, which has been sensed through a negative effect on their lives. A variety of expressions for spiritual and church renewal abound, and they usually are legitimate avenues of renewal for God's people. For countless thousands, liturgical renewal, charismatic renewal, and experiences such as Faith Alive and Marriage Encounter, to name only a few of these forms, have meant an encounter with God that is beginning to fill the spiritual vacuums in their lives and to produce some positive results in life.

Cults generally offer a style of life and sense of purpose and spiritual fulfillment that appears to be alive, everlasting, and genuine. A person "looking in" on a cult would perceive people who appear happy, spiritually fulfilled, and knowing deep purpose for their lives. Many cults will appeal to the person who has a keen sense of righteousness or morality, as well as a vulnerable emotional state. It is not unusual to hear cults also attempt to fulfill the patriotic needs of their memberships through the expression of usually conservative political viewpoints and special events such as one group's Bicentennial "God Bless America" event in July 1976.

SOME MEMBERS SEEK A SENSE OF ESCAPE

The "drug culture of the sixties" may soon be replaced by the "cult culture of the eighties," where people gather to seek easy answers to hard questions or to totally escape the reality of life in favor of some profferred dream world. Whether motivated by a sense of escapism or the desire to work for a better world, these people are certainly drawn to the "pie in the sky" promises that some groups make.

But the need to escape is, in part, fostered by conditions in society that lie far beyond the influence or control of the potential cult member. A recent U.S. Department of Labor survey showed that almost 42 percent of the people in the general age group most susceptible to cults (eighteen to twenty-five years) desired to seek a job that carried with it some professional status or to work in a helping profession; that same survey showed that only 17 percent of that total group who desired such goals in life could ever hope to find satisfying jobs or vocations. Those unfulfilled desires are the seedbed of frustration and disillusionment; if these people are not effectively helped in finding constructive redirection for their lives, the implication is that a great number of America's next generation of leaders may bear some significant degree of dissatisfaction with their life's work. This sort of tension makes the cult's offer of commitment and service even more appealing. This problem is not merely statistical or theoretical; there are thousands of people vulnerable to cults who have spent many years and thousands of dollars to attain a level of specialized training that would allow them to function in a chosen profession; some of these same people are doing unskilled manual labor because of job shortages, while others are chronically unemployed because they are overeducated for the positions available. There is little chance of escaping frustration in a cycle like this, in which the age-old adage of "hard work will lead to success" is no longer valid.

SOME NEED A SENSE OF COMMUNITY

Most people experience some degree of motivation to belong to some organization or group. We join groups to establish our identities, to improve ourselves, to gain friends, to serve others, or even for recreation. Cults offer such a group experience in an atmosphere where the aura of friendship prevails and offers a cohesiveness that encourages a sense of security for individual members.

SOME SUFFER A SENSE OF ALIENATION

As mentioned earlier, people who are on the verge of a new life situation, whether in education, the military, or work, are especially vulnerable to the recruiting efforts of cults. These people may be undergoing some feelings of alienation; however temporary or predicated by immediate circumstances those feelings may be, they are still very real.

It is, however, significant to note that many cults are adept at creating a feeling of alienation where none had previously existed. Certain cults claim to draw families together, but evidence drawn from their internal propaganda suggests exactly the opposite; they are not adverse to referring to their own group as the "true family" that cares for the individual. One group's leader, while publicly expressing a desire for family unity, actually sees such unity existing only within his own group. "You must separate yourself from your satanic environment. . . . You have to cut off the environment of your physical parents, and even the fallen husband and wife relationships."[5] Using a generalized concept of evil in the world, the cults often influence young adults to view their natural families, who perhaps do not fully support this new-found religious activity, as evil; therefore, the natural family should be forsaken for the welfare of the cult and the spiritual safety of the individual member.

Cults can use geography to heighten alienation. Some groups perform their indoctrination in remote areas, far removed from other indications of civilization. In these locations, the cults can maintain a close watch over potential members and new recruits, manipulating almost every word or thought that might enter their heads. One group with a recruiting center in northern California has been accused by a number of former members of such manipulation and supervision. Recruitees' rights to private telephone conversations with their parents were constantly violated because some older member of the group was constantly present during such attempted conversations.[6]

Cults are able to use geography to put distance between members and their families even after membership is assumed. If a family is trying to reach a cult member in a particular city, and the cult judges the family to be hostile to its purposes, it is a simple matter to move the cult member quickly and quietly to another cult center, even to another continent. Some groups have resorted to this technique in order to prevent conservatorship papers being served on members.

Probably the most difficult means of creating alienation, but also the most effective, is to create cultural differences. Most cults' members look, dress, and act like normal people; whether this is reality or only appearance is a question we will face later. But certain groups do maintain a cultural image that demands "something extra" of the convert. It is one thing to solicit funds in a railroad station while wearing a three-piece vested suit and quite a different matter to perform the same activity while wearing long robes and with a shaved head. The ability of some groups to use such unfamiliar cultural features in their methodology only works to increase the already obvious "we-they" nature of the group. Not only does such a cultural difference identify the group to the observer, but it also reinforces the cult member's apparent spiritual distinctiveness from the world.

SOME NEED AN AUTHORITY FIGURE

Wouldn't life be easier if only someone else would make all your decisions for you? Many people feel that way, and some cults are adept at meeting that need for authority over a person's life. Some cults meet this need by demanding blind obedience and total dependency by members toward the leadership. One cult leader says it well: "I am your brain. . . . I am the leader of your group, in the place of God. . . . I am happy when I am enjoying a position higher than other people."[7]

Others seek a structure where behavioral guidelines are carefully enumerated. Their desire is for a legalistic structure that carefully delineates the rightness of certain forms of behavior. Another type of person, deprived of strong parental figures, may simply desire a relationship with an organization or an individual who cares enough about him to take the trouble to guide and to correct. At least two major cult figures refer to their followers as "my kids," which reinforces naturally enough the image of the father figure. Could it be possible that permissive child rearing has helped to spawn the attractiveness of cults?

SOME FEEL THAT "THE CHURCH" HAS FAILED THEM

It is evident from the cult phenomenon that contact with organized religion is not enough to insure a secure relationship with God. One parent of a cult member stated that their children had "never been religious before, although I had taken them regularly to Episcopal Church Sunday school classes when they were little." The passive attitudes of some parents, which allow their children to grow up without a formative experience of religious traditions and values has led to a generation of children who have little or no ability to recognize a real religion. "We want our children to be able to make their own choice of religion" may be a beautiful sentiment, but unless the parents provide a basis for comparison, the children may, at best, be drawn to the most attractively packaged religion. Could it be that too many parents make that sort of statement, appearing to be "open minded" with their children, when in fact the parents themselves have little or no substantive religious background to share with their children?

Ignorance of the Bible and the "failure of the church" to teach people how to pray draws many people to cults; these inductees know that they have a spiritual side to their lives that has remained undernourished, if not famished. Some observers claim that cult members are drawn primarily from nonreligious backgrounds, seeking not religion but the "fruits of religious experience," such as peace, happiness, and self-fulfillment.[8] However, both informal studies and reports from former members have indicated that the religious backgrounds of cult members often bear close connections to traditional religions; while no exact statistics are available, it is apparent, if only from a sampling of those who have left their cult participation, that people from Jewish, Roman Catholic, and Protestant backgrounds are all vulnerable to some degree. If the cults were not a significant problem, would the Jewish community or other religious bodies be so concerned about losing members to these groups? It is interesting to note that some observers have reported an apparently disproportionately smaller percentage of cult members coming from conservative Protestant backgrounds; presumably, these people may have enjoyed a deeper indoctrination into the Bible and may therefore be better equipped to deal with some of the spurious biblical teachings.

While some leaders and spokesmen for traditional religious groups feel that the cult experience emerges from an egocentric turning inward, topped off by a religious "quick fix," it is also true that those attracted to cults often have a negative set of feelings directed toward traditional religions. For some, their experience has resulted in personal hurt when people who claimed to be loving fell far short of the individual's expectations. Others perhaps are troubled by the apparent lack of concern for social issues that some organized religions have shown, or by the turmoil that seems to arise over internal conflicts centering on doctrines and dogmas.

Many cults readily respond to the possible negative feelings of recruits toward traditional religions by reinforcing the picture of organized, traditional religion offering hollow phrases and creating a spiritual vacuum, which only the cult can fill. While extremely critical of all other religions, these groups each claim to offer to mankind the one true religion. They stress the allegedly apparent weaknesses of traditional religion: Jesus Christ was a failure, people do not take the

Bible seriously, all regular Christians are hypocrites. The apparently "fresh" approach of some cults, which all too often is only either a recycled heresy or the workings of a megalomaniac, would obviously be appealing to many who are disillusioned by institutional religion as expressed in traditional Judaism and Christianity.

One spokesman for a prominent new religion, which some consider an extremely dangerous cult of almost five hundred thousand people, feels that young people will soon be expressing not only dissatisfaction with traditional religions but perhaps even with the newer religions themselves; he feels that they will start to seek a second generation of religious highs. Young people will continue to make rapid changes in religious affiliation because their lives are changing far faster than stable religions can change to keep up with them.

Will the cult experience snowball into new and even stranger forms of religion, as this one prophet predicts? Or has this prophet perhaps been late in his appraisal of the situation? If the customary trend of new cultural and spiritual fads beginning in California holds true, then the second dawning of the people who are able to invent their own religion and draw converts has already occurred in Los Angeles.[9] Condemning not only traditional, orthodox religions as valueless and hypocritical, one group has also lashed out at the cults, while offering itself as the freshly emerging spiritual vanguard of the future:

THE GREAT RELIGIOUS RIP-OFF

You are a victim! No matter what your religious persuasion—or lack of—your life is affected by orthodox religion. The atmosphere of your entire society is regulated by its influence. This world-wide assault is being perpetrated by hundreds of denominations and thousands of localized churches. . . . Billions of dollars a year are being extracted from trusting, but gullible, peo-

ple who are seeking salvation. This money is used to
further reinforce erroneous teachings about Jesus, the
Bible, and the origin and destiny of humankind. . . .
Our need is too great! No longer can the good works
and good intentions of orthodox religions be allowed to
justify the untruths being taught. It is the end of the
Church Age. But now we face an even greater
challenge. There is the ever-present danger that it will
be replaced by something even less viable. Our society is
besieged by all sorts of cults and "New Age" religions.
Most of them are phony, if not downright dangerous.
Our powers of discernment are now put to the test. We
must seek new definitions of self, life, and God. We
must free ourselves of irrelevant dogmas that blunt our
awareness and stifle our understanding. Christ showed
us the way. His message was simple—to change and
transform ourselves through love for each other and love
for God. The Crucifixion serves as the ultimate symbol
of this necessary transformation. Change, from ordinary
humanness to something greater than human—a sacred
being, compatible with the glory of the coming Kingdom.

Naturally, this second-generation cult invites the curious
to attend its meetings at a theater rented for such gatherings
in downtown Los Angeles every Sunday; in addition, information about membership or training programs can be received easily by contacting the given telephone number or
visiting the group's office. Whether the "life system" this
group offers to "experience the power of love in action" with
others who seek spiritually in a "common quest for enlightenment" is simply another cult or something less pernicious
remains to be seen. However, many of the cult appeals and
techniques, including the appeals to idealistic people, the
put-down of institutional churches, and offers of the opportunity to change from ordinary humanness to something special leave room for speculation as to the basic nature of the
group. In fact, this group even transcends the most radical

first-generation cults by promising people that they can become greater than human, "a sacred being, compatible with
the glory of the coming Kingdom," which is rather fantastic
in itself! What could be a greater ego trip to offer the public?

chapter 3

Why Cults Have Flourished

The first question about cults that people often ask is "Why are the cults experiencing such a high degree of apparent success in their recruitment? After all, aren't our kids still in favor of baseball, hot dogs, and apple pie?" While this line of inquiry appears to be simple, the answers it evokes are quite diverse, reflecting a startling analysis of the society we live in and the tottering foundations on which some of our cultural ideals rest. Social evolution in the United States has kept abreast of even the radical observations Alvin Toffler made in 1970 with *Future Shock*.[1]

People in America are losing the significance of the individual while we focus our attention more and more on the welfare of the masses. We are saturated with media reports that proclaim new, troubling problems, each of which suggests its own doomsday effect; military and political conflicts, pollution, inflation, and conservation of energy have joined nuclear weapons as signposts that lead to our culture's Armageddon.

We all know people who are increasingly lonely, although these very people may seldom be alone. If you ride a bus on almost any municipal transportation system, you will gaze into empty stares, if you can even meet another person's eye. Those stares seem to grow even emptier with each passing year. Even the materialistic impulses of our society have given rise to loneliness through the increase of "leisure time," whether through incentives for early retirement, increased holidays, or even the four-day work week. People have increasingly sought diversion or escape, in part because they are not as urgently needed at their work or in their families.

That "age of Aquarius," which was heralded in the late 1960s, brought with it a "high" society that differed radically from the swing era of the 1920s, the euphoria and relief of the years following World War II, or even the tranquility of the late 1950s. "Human potential" became the cry of many who sought a new identity in the counterculture movements. "Trips" became more than a vacation journey to the mountains or the beach as millions of young and old alike "turned on" to the latest psychedelic drugs or prescription medications while they thronged to movie theaters to see reruns of *Fantasia,* the harmless animated fantasy which became for many a symbol of the drug culture. High-school students have learned how to manufacture "angel dust" in the basements of their homes, enabling them to experience the latest psychedelic crutch for escape whenever they don't like the way the world looks. People have sought higher and higher peaks or increasingly exciting experiences. Where could it go to next?

Our American culture is shifting from the age of medication to the era of meditation. The country that consumes record amounts of tranquilizers every year is turning toward spiritual experience, both traditional and new, legitimate and fraudulent. Some have been smart enough to evolve a technology for the spiritual realm of man, where religious and psychological philosophies have been interwoven and successfully marketed to many thousands of curious seekers. The range of appeal of such new religions is wide, spanning the spectrum from spiritual enlightenment to restored lives, from mail-order ordinations that allow for tax write-offs on property to the ability to dematerialize your body and float through a wall.

The results of all these phenomena can be laden with disaster. Human potential movements, religious experiences, and even the drug culture have combined forces to produce an entire segment of society that is totally egocentric. "What's in it for me?" is the prevailing question, whether in welfare applications or job interviews. People have become more concerned about how many days of vacation they will have this year than in what kind of work they might be doing in a new job!

Many people are wearied of the constant bombardment by change; future shock has become a chronic illness for millions. These people seek security and simplicity, and perhaps rightly so. However, some people resist change simply because they do not desire to face a new challenge. What could be a more respectable means of escaping the challenge of social change than to "become religious"? Many new religious groups have packaged their products to appeal to exactly this type of person, who is feeling almost unbearable pressures from his ordinary, daily life-style.

But even as a new generation of Americans emerges from an era of violence in the streets, political assassinations, corruption in government, and countless other disillusioning stresses, there are several other factors in social evolution that are easily demonstrated and have offered some contribution to the increase in religious activity in America, whether in new religious "cults" or even old religions in new packages.

INCREASED GEOGRAPHIC MOBILITY

The 1970 U.S. census reported that some 20 percent of American families move every year; even this relatively high figure is a low estimate eight years later for certain areas of the country and some segments of the population. The continual uprooting of families places a harsh strain on all its members. Children, however, are most often the most affected members of a family. They lose opportunities to develop lasting peer relationships; they are continually thrown into new systems of moral and personal expectations with their peers. Furthermore, their educational process may be disrupted seriously. Even a shift of neighborhoods within one small city can create a sociological trauma as devastating as a move across the continent.

Describing this phenomenon among the members of one group that he investigated, Harvard University theologian Harvey Cox reports that cult members are often seeking simple human friendships. One member told him that a cult cared for him, clearing his personal confusion while also offering a sense of identity. Even though the outward appearances and behavior of the group was threatening, the member now feels he is "an important part" of this group, "where I was meant to be." The group offered friendship and a sense of identity; the offer was accepted.[2]

Technological advances in transportation have allowed cult leaders and even cult members to invest their financial resources in means of insuring increased geographic mobility. If a group needs members in a distant city for a special project, the leaders simply gather a group for the "mission" and fly them, perhaps in the cult's private jet airplane, wherever they must go. Cult leaders are quite adept at the effective use of modern technology for the spread of their messages, whether through the media or by flying around the country, or even the world, to visit far-flung disciples.

DISINTEGRATION OF THE EXTENDED FAMILY

Young people are coming to the realization at an increasingly earlier age that their parents are not eternal, omnipresent sources of love and security. The discovery is not new, nor is it necessarily bad. The problem is that young adults are discovering these aspects of their parents at ages when they are not yet totally equipped to deal with this discovery. "Who am I?" becomes a pressing question at an earlier age, but the answer is not to be found as a member of the family but rather as an individual who has asserted his independence from the nuclear family.

The stress on nuclear family life is severe. Divorce rates have never been higher, nor do they show any indication of decreasing; the methods for obtaining "quick divorces" have never been more readily available to all portions of society. Some attribute the increase in divorce rates to a shift in moral standards; others contend, and rightly so, that economic pressures have contributed to the failure of many marriages. Families that once enjoyed well-defined social and economic roles between husband and wife have been subjected to the pressures of maintaining or reaching a standard of living that has created a chasm between spouses.

Even our leisure society has added to family stress. How many families gather around the table for a daily common meal and to communicate the events and feelings of the day? Do we stress time for family activity and togetherness, or are driving lessons, dancing class, and football more important? The number of families who consciously make the effort to bind their members together in a common life shrinks as we rush out to bowling leagues, service organizations, self-improvement classes, and even church meetings.

Even the way that nuclear families treat their prior generations has helped add to the insecurity of young people about their family ties. Today, young people see their grandparents or other aged relatives being placed in institutional settings, which are designed for what is little more than custodial care; the young people know that such care could often be provided at home, if anyone cared enough. Consequently, children are not only deprived of the experience of growing up around older people but also threatened by the prospect of their own process of growing old in an institution.

NORMAL GROWTH PROBLEMS
OF ADOLESCENCE

The great majority of cult members, but by no means all members, fall into the eighteen to twenty-five age range. It follows that people emerging from adolescence into adult-hood are most susceptible.

Early adulthood, which extends until around age thirty, is characteristically a time of personal uncertainty; in fact, some observers believe that the age limits of adolescence must be redefined upward to include those closer to age thirty. "Whom will I marry, if anyone at all?" "What will be my life's work?" "Who am I and what are my goals?" are questions that assail young adults in a steady onslaught; most freshmen in college are expected to select their college major when they first register for classes, without even the opportunity to expand their intellectual and personal horizons beyond what may be only high-school professional fantasies. People in this age group are susceptible to feelings of insignificance about their lives; they endure a continual struggle simply to recognize their own importance. Drug abuse may be most severe at this stage of development, and the possibility of suicide is a serious option for some young adults.

The cults can understand these transition problems as well as we can, and their programs and approaches are often designed to offer "pie in the sky" solutions to these problems that often bewilder young adults.

ELECTRONIC MEDIA

Too many critics are calling television *the* source of all our problems; nothing could be less true. While television is not *the* source of cultural and sociological upheaval in America, it does deserve some close scrutiny to determine whether it is *a* major source of social evolution, and even disintegration, in America. Does the fact that, by age eighteen, an American youth has spent a significant portion of his waking hours watching television have a harmful effect on that individual? Does it matter that he is being entertained most of the time, rather than learning to discover and to evaluate for himself? Does it matter that by age eighteen the average television viewer will have viewed over three thousand acts of violence on television? On the dust jacket of *The Plug-In Drug,* Marie Winn writes that our society is dominated by television, "of children with poor verbal skills, an inability to concentrate, and a disinclination to read, of parents who are 'hooked' on using the television as a sedative for their preschool children."[3]

AMERICA MAY BECOME A THIRD WORLD STATE

Political upheavals, economic advantages, and adventure are three forces that still motivate people to immigrate, often illegally, to the United States. We Americans must consider the fact that an increasing number of new residents of this great land come from countries or ethnic groups that are "strange" to many of us. Walk through a large shopping center in southern California or metropolitan New York and you will see, with each passing year, that increasing proportions of the faces are nonwhite and nonblack.

While this country has always represented opportunity to countless millions of people from other lands, will we be able to absorb so many different customs and traditions, as well as religions, in our society? The cults are often a part of this influx of new cultures, as expressions of eastern religious philosophies become more prevalent in America. It is quite possible that, within a few years, "white America" will be in the minority in the sociological structures of some states; in fact, "white America" and "black America" eventually may not be able to combine their influence to represent a majority voice in the country. Can we adjust to that and accept this new social and political status? Or, as this matter relates to the questions surrounding new religions, will those of us who have been nourished in our predominantly Jewish-Christian heritage, regardless of race or national origin, be able to live in a radically heterogeneous society, where we might no longer, by majority vote, be "one nation under God"?

chapter 4

How Do Cults Recruit?

No group can continue to grow without new members, and the new religions are extremely adept at recruiting potential members through a wide variety of means. Posters on dormitory walls proclaim YOU CAN BE A WINNER, overcoming all of life's problems if you will only take a particular Bible-study course! Flyers distributed in the San Francisco area challenge young people to rise to the cause of righteousness:

> Are you ready to accept the challenge of a new age? If so, we are really anxious to meet you. . . . Let's join hands together to build a better world.

In areas where major college campuses are scattered, newspaper ads can serve the same purpose. These two ads appeared recently in a midwestern newspaper and refer to the same group:

SPIRITUAL ADVENTURE AND A GOOD TIME.
SPEND A WEEKEND AT A NEW LIFE WORKSHOP.
CALL GREG. [number listed]

A CHRISTIAN PEACE CORPS . . .
HAS OPENINGS BOTH HERE AND ABROAD.
ARE YOU 18 TO 25? CALL [number listed]

Parents familiar with the group sponsoring these two advertisements protested to the newspaper and successfully persuaded the publisher to agree to the screening of all such material before publication. But the damage already might have been done. A blind invitation was given, designed to draw the unsuspecting, idealistic young adult into an experience that he might neither anticipate nor perhaps freely withdraw from.

There are two variables that lead to successful recruiting for a cult; these variables are no different from any effective sales technique used by other organizations and businesses. First, the person approached must be vulnerable to "purchasing" the product. Some cults make a concerted recruiting effort directed toward people with some obvious weakness that might make them open to the sales approach of the recruiter, often called the "witnesser." College campuses at the beginning of each semester are fertile grounds for religious recruitment among people who are newly arrived and somewhat unsettled about their surroundings. They have been uprooted perhaps from a familiar background for the first time ever, and therefore they may be eager to gravitate toward any offer of personal interest or friendship. Street recruiters are trained to watch for people with signs of restlessness or mobility; young people with guitars or backpacks in the midst of large cities are excellent recruiting prospects.[1]

The second variable to be considered is the level of saturation. The opportunity to accomplish a successful recruiting encounter increases for the cult in direct proportion to the increased number of cult recruiters on the streets. This is so true that on some street corners several members of a cult will gather and approach people coming at them from all directions; it is this style of "saturation selling" that often proves to be quite successful.

The street approach that stresses "increased human under-standing" and "building a better world" is most successful for certain groups. One young man found himself involved in a major pseudo-Christian cult almost by accident. His story is typical of the recruiting experiences of many people who have joined a cult for what might be called "the weekend that never ends."

The name of the operation sounded innocent enough. I thought it was a group of industrious and creative peo-ple who were organizing to build something beneficial to mankind. That is the impression which people from the "Operation" are trying to convey. That sounds im-pressive, of course.

Recruiters for the "Operation" claim it to be a well-organized group of intellectuals who want to bring love back to mankind. One thing which they do not mention is that they are followers of . . . and that the "Opera-tion" is a part of. . . . The name "Operation" is merely a front. If one asks anybody from the "family" (as they call themselves) if they are associated with the (parent group), they will flatly deny it.

My existence had been that of a starving artist. I spent much time painting and exhibiting my work at art shows. My experience with the "family" began at an outdoor art show in San Francisco where I was exhibit-ing. A pleasant young woman approached me and asked me how I got into art. I told her that I had begun to work on a master's degree in psychology, but I was turned off by the "rat running" and statistics and dropped out to pursue my art. It happened that she had a master's in psychology and had worked for her doctor-ate at Berkeley and had dropped out for the same rea-sons. So we talked for a while and she finally told me that she was with a "community project." She said they had a house in the city and that they had dinner and meetings there. She invited me to dinner and would not take "no" for an answer. So I said that I would think about it. I really did not have anything to do that evening, so I decided to go. It turned out that the lady who invited me to dinner was the director of this so-called "Operation." It was considered a tremendous honor to be invited by Catherine.

Dinner was followed by the "Operation's" introductory lecture, given by Catherine. The lecture focused on how distant people can be from one another and how often we lack love in our loves. All this seemed to make sense, and anyone not satisfied with his life might be likely to have his interest aroused. Many young people are not totally unhappy with their lives, so "the family" can appeal to people of many walks of life.

Later a talk was given about a farm that the "family" owns (out in the country in northern California). The speaker said that [at the farm] they have seminars which explain what the "Operation" is all about. Slides were shown and I saw what a beautiful place the farm is. The implication of this talk was that the farm is a place to go and get your head together and have a peaceful time of fun and frolic. So the idea is planted in the visitor's mind that the farm is an ideal place to vacation and have good, clean fun. Any idea that this might be some form of religious community is carefully concealed.

All the people in the "family" seemed very open and friendly. What really struck me was how much the "family" members smiled and how happy they appeared. Not being very satisfied with my own life, I thought that it would be a very good idea if I went to the farm.[2]

Two interesting recruitment techniques jump out of this testimony. First of all, the recruiter established a relationship with the prospect and immediately adopted an identity similar to the prospect's; by coincidence, Catherine's background did happen to resemble the artist's. However, if the prospect had been a dropout from medical school, Catherine would have presented herself as one too. Her reputation as a master at such deception is well known among members of her group. Also note the importance given to the person offering the invitation. It was an "honor" to be invited by the director; such remarks are obviously designed to build up the ego state of the prospective member as he starts to enjoy his new-found friends, all of whom smile readily at him and will exhibit interest in his life's story at every opportunity.

The basic marketing technique of a cult is the appeal to human need; almost everyone wants to feel important, to be both loved and lovable, as well as loving others. The cults direct their recruitment efforts towards these basic human needs, using an approach that proves compelling to many. There are at least eight aspects of recruitment that are held in common, to some degree, by the major cults.

MEMBERS ARE TRAINED TO RECRUIT

There is nothing unusual about a religion wanting to develop some approach for sharing its faith; in Christian traditions, the approach is usually considered some form of evangelism. The cults are no different; they train members for the dissemination of their own religious views. However, their approaches are much more thorough. What the potential inductee senses is a genuine love directed towards him as a unique individual whom the recruiter appreciates. However, this guise of love is often no more than a carefully designed witnessing ritual, which is effectively executed.

One major organization has an instruction manual for witnessing, which includes sections on how to make friends, what sorts of topics might be discussed, how often to contact your prospect (including favorable times of day for greatest receptivity), and how to integrate the prospect into the cult group through local peer fellowships, which are often disguised as "nonsectarian" Bible studies or groups of people who share similar concerns.[3]

Another group holds sexual contact with potential

members as a valid and effective recruiting tool. "Flirty fish" of both sexes are sent out to places where they can best ply their trade. The group tells its members: "Eye contact is very important. Give 'em a look of love and watch their hearts turn out. Watch your breath! Be sure to brush your teeth and use mints. You can blow away a lot of potential 'givers.' Try hopping a school bus and asking the kids if they want to go to heaven. . . . Pray with them and don't forget to leave some literature with them before you hop off. . . . At a concert or a high school when kids are moving fast it often helps to shorten your speech to 'can you help with change for kids?' or 'Any change for kids?' When you mention children it really touches people's hearts and encourages better donations. You should enjoy *litnessing* as much as lovemaking." (*Litnessing* is both listening and witnessing.) This group stresses giving potential converts the "look of love"; "If there is real spiritual contact in a look it's just like getting into bed naked with someone." Flirty fish are expected to file regular reports on their sexual encounters, in effect, prostitution for proselytizing. In addition to basic statistical information on the number of encounters made, the level of sexual involvement and its effectiveness for *litnessing* is reported on the back side of the report, as well as the explicit details of the most interesting sexual encounter of the past month.[4] Local groups are then expected to provide a cost analysis of the sexual exploits of its members, including cost-per-encounter and the effective rate of return, in terms of actual converts, for each dollar spent.

REINFORCEMENT AND INTEGRATION OF PERSONAL GOALS

Cult recruiters will often center an initial conversation with the prospect around that person's goals, visions for the world, or philosophical foundations. (Note that this happened in the case study above, although that was a rare instance where the interests happened to coincide.) The inevitable response, whether honest or deceitful, is "Yes, I agree with you completely, and I know some people who feel exactly as we do. Would you like to join us some evening to share our common concerns?"

Once the bait is taken, the group opens itself to the prospect and shares the same type of reinforcement technique. Initially a fascination with the individual's thoughts and goals is expressed, only to diminish as the integration processes continue and the group begins to share its own value system with the potential convert.

STRONG PEER PRESSURE

The integration of personal goals is but one portion of a broader effort to provide *peer approval*. Remember that cults tend to seek out people who are in a transitional stage of life, whose self-image may not be well formed yet. Suddenly the awkward teen-ager, off to college and away from home for the first time, meets people who actually appear to like him, pimples and all, and who also appear to be eager to invest something of themselves in him.

Once this foundation has been laid, the cult will reverse the process and begin to use *peer pressure* to keep a person involved with the group and committed to the cause. The effect on the inductee is profitable to the cult in many instances; he asks himself, "These people have accepted me as I am, and they have been good to me. Don't I therefore have an obligation to work at meeting their expectations of me? After all, I want to be loved and to feel respect." While this might not be the most appropriate question to raise at this point in time, it is a common question which emerges in one form or another before a deeper commitment to the group can be made.

According to pyschiatrist Robert Lifton, the basic techniques of recruitment and maintaining interest contribute to the loss of judgment and authority:

> I would emphasize that these coercive psychological
> and physical methods tend to be accompanied by
> various forms of deception concerning the purposes of
> the cult, which the disciple is at first unaware of and
> later unable to confront because of his loss of critical
> judgment and autonomy.[5]

Lifton has described concisely the phenomenon that
hundreds of cult recruits have encountered, including a reporter for the *New York Daily News,* who sought to infiltrate
a well-known group and report to his readership on its alleged methods of manipulation. In late 1975, a reporter
allowed himself to be recruited by a major cult in front of the
New York Public Library, on the fringes of Manhattan's
Times Square area; this would be a thorough effort at observation, for he was a trained professional journalist, college
educated and street wise, and also a very conservative, practicing Roman Catholic. Having some knowledge of how to
make himself vulnerable, the reporter set himself up to be
approached with an invitation to view a movie about the
group, which was shown in an office several doors away.
After he was invited and viewed the film, the reporter was
encouraged to attend a weekend retreat at a house in the
Queens section of New York. When he arrived early Friday
evening for his weekend experience, the reporter was
ushered into a Victorian frame, three-story home in good condition and in a respectable neighborhood. But there was only
one problem: the house was populated that weekend with
over forty-five people, including the forty recruits who had
decided to accept their invitation!

The opening session lasted well into the early hours of the
morning; singing and discussion were mixed with presen-
tations from the leaders about major issues confronting
the world today. When "lights out" finally came around
1:30 A.M., the men were herded into the basement while

the women were segregated on another floor. There was only one functioning bathroom for the entire house, so people had little opportunity for comfortable use of toilet facilities.

Wake-up was sounded shortly after 5:00 A.M. when a weekend leader entered to arouse anyone who had been able to rest in the open sleeping areas by urging them to sing. Once again, the scene from the previous evening was repeated when the lines formed quickly at the bathroom; the men had no opportunity to shave and no one had an adequate opportunity to bathe during the course of the weekend. Some morning exercises and songs were followed by the first of six meals served over the weekend, which were the classic menus needed for inducing the weariness and weakness that must precede coercive persuasion. Meals were always filling and seemed satisfying, but they were devoid of the basic nutritional requirements that normal adults require. Most foods served were high in starch and carbohydrates while low in protein value. Everything offered was tasty and filling, but not necessarily adequate to meet the bodily needs of the recruits.

The *Daily News* reporter discovered that it was not until well into the second day of meetings that any discussions that focused on religion were brought into the foreground by the leaders. But as the afternoon unfolded, teachings centered on the group's unique scriptures were expounded to the recruits, whose attention spans were shortening, while the combination of poor diet and lack of sufficient sleep combined with the generally dirty feeling of bodies, which were uncleaned and unshaven for two days. This two-fold manipulation is essential to controlling a person's thoughts: wear the subject down, preferably without his consent or awareness of the process happening, while building up the information you want the subject to eventually accept.

Sunday's activities followed the same pattern as Saturday's for the recruits, with the sole exception that the religious overtones of the weekend grew increasingly more blatant. But, by this time, many were exhausted and ready to give in to almost anything they heard. These forty people had endured a classic pattern of *antagonism, apathy,* and *acceptance*. The antagonism phase may appear quite placid on the surface; but in the hearer's mind, there are thoughts that dispel any quick acceptance of the group's positions. As weariness sets in, so does the apathy; there is a feeling of "just coasting along" with what is happening, perhaps looking forward to the conclusion but not being quite as critical. It is at this point that the religious teachings can be effectively introduced. The third stage, acceptance, comes commonly sometime on Sunday, when the subject is most worn down; acceptance of almost anything that these people suggest has become highly probable. Deprivation of physical essentials and emotional degradation are coupled with peer pressure and increasingly dogmatic teachings to bring about what the cult leaders hope will be a conversion to the group.

As unreal as this type of weekend might seem to most people, it does happen with many cults. On this particular weekend, the reporter could have slipped out of the house and abandoned the entire project; however, the staggering outcome of the weekend was its effect on the reporter. This trained professional, an articulate Christian, stated at the end of his report that had the weekend lasted only a few hours longer, his own resistance to the group and its techniques would have been so worn down that he might have committed himself to the group.[6]

Not everyone who underwent this type of weekend experience was as lucky as the reporter from New York. The same group runs a recruitment center in northern California where inductees are bussed, often from hundreds of miles away, to a location with no readily accessible public transportation. They might be allowed to walk away (although this is debated by many) or they can wait until the group is ready to return them. While the group has made continuing claims that recruiting techniques have been improved over the years, the indication is that much room is needed still for more improvement.[7] The value of preventative education can be shown in the experience of a Canadian couple who met this group in San Francisco and escaped less scathed than many from the trap set for them.

> A little more than a year ago my fiancée and I were passing through San Francisco. . . . Neither of us had heard of the cult leader or the "Operation," so being invited to dinner by a couple of friendly fellows on Fisherman's Wharf seemed like a harmless prospect. . . . We bit the bait very carefully. We consented to go to the farm, provided we could go in our own vehicle. . . . On arrival at the farm, we were each assigned a "watchdog," who was responsible for keeping us as far apart as possible for the entire weekend. Our continuous attempts to foil these guards not only helped to keep our minds perked, but also revealed to us the meticulous planning that must have been going on behind the scenes. A soft-sell approach to convincing a visitor to stay was the continual assurance that the answers to all questions would come in tomorrow's lectures, and that the lecturer was so much more qualified. The hard-sell methods were saved until the end of the weekend, by which time the most desirable visitors had been singled out and the hard-core members sicked on them. . . . . . My girl friend was already told that I had committed myself to stay another week, and I was told it was perfectly justifiable to abandon her right there and then, to commit myself to this only true (though undefined) life . . . .

This couple was fortunate; they escaped because they were aware of the dangers that might be present and they maintained a suspicious mind-set.[8]

Still another form of peer pressure reflects an ancient

heresy that has often risen to the surface within Christian tradition. Many cults concentrate on the *gnostic concepts* of good and evil in the world. Whenever a member may be gravitating toward connections with the world outside of the religion, the leaders, often appearing as concerned peers, will use a simple argument that sways many. "You feel that our group has holy people in it and that we are the Truth. People outside our group disagree with us; therefore, these people are not as holy as we are. If they fail to meet our holiness because they reject the Truth and may even violently oppose it, then the devil must have some sort of hold on them." While the cult members who offer this style of advice often appear to be concerned peers, they may be nothing more, as some allege, than cult-manufactured authority figures, whose responsibility is to project concepts of "us and them," which will be further reinforced by other members. Peer pressure is vital in instilling a feeling of "other worldliness," but it is much more effective when accompanied by the added factor of authority: "Well, the leader says it; therefore it must be true."

Peer pressure may be used to break a recruit's inquisitive or suspicious nature. Rather than allow free inquiry, some cults resort to watching each member so that negative thoughts cannot be expressed or allowed to develop. One young woman discovered that her new religion frowned on such questioning and took actions to prevent this from happening:

> I soon learned that the baby Christians were not to ask any probing questions about group affairs, but patiently wait until events were officially announced by Pastors and overseers. The common answer to curious inquiries was "None of your business" or "Stop being a busybody." If the new follower persisted in asking too many questions, the Pastors and overseers would label that person a "troublemaker" and watch them closely.[9]

CULTS KNOW THEIR MARKETS

The people most prone to accepting a cultic invitation are those who, in the midst of transition, are confronted with a major crisis or change in life-style. We have seen already how one cult member recently had turned away from his educational career and was struggling to survive as a young artist. As mentioned earlier, people on college campuses are especially vulnerable at the beginning of their first semester on campus or just before graduation; they must face a new, and probably uncomfortable, environment, stripped of former friends, the security of home or campus, and perhaps even stripped of financial security. What happens when a person undergoing this magnitude of turmoil is offered "spiritual blessings to answer all the questions of life" or "how to whip the devil"? The answer is simple: He will be sorely tempted to investigate such an offer, or at least more tempted than at most other times of his life.

Street witnessing includes the careful eye, which watches for signs of mobility or other indications of need. Young people with backpacks are vulnerable to aggressive recruiting; the chances for a recruiting encounter increase if the recruiter senses that his prospect might have money to contribute. One group, which has survived as a cult offshoot of the "Jesus Movement" of the late 1960s, found a very successful place to market its religion: in and around the counseling centers of colleges and universities. Rather than using random selection as a means of finding people with problems or who were searching, the group went to where these people gathered. It proved to be a simple matter to stand outside the counseling center and to solicit patients or clients about their religious needs as they emerged from counseling sessions.

CULTS OFFER COMMITMENT AND SERVICE

Most new religions proclaim that they are seeking to make life better for people through some type of service-oriented activity. One prominent group working in San Francisco has a front organization that claims to be offering community service projects to a number of institutions; the group even lists a number of highly respectable and traditional agencies at which its members allegedly assist, including a Salvation Army hospital. The only difficulty, as we saw earlier, was that Salvation Army officials were not aware that this group was claiming that its members worked at the hospital or that the group was a front organization for a cult whose theology is totally contrary to the strongly Christian tenets of the Salvation Army. In fact, the Salvation Army denied that the group had any contact at all with their hospital.[10]

"Missions" are an important part of cult recruiting. Groups may offer their prospective converts many possibilities for service, including educational work, drug rehabilitation, and other worthwhile causes. What these groups often do not reveal is that most "missions" involve fund raising to support the cult organization and its leader. In fact, the same group that claimed the connection mentioned above with a Salvation Army hospital recently filed suit against seven cities in southern California to protest their licensing laws. What was confusing was the contrast between all the claims of worthwhile service that this group does and their own description of their primary work as "proselytizing and fund raising," "the very mainstay" of their religious movement. There was no allusion given to a relationship with God or the performance of socially beneficial deeds mentioned in their primary purpose, according to newspaper reports.[11]

Little, if any, of the funds collected by some groups go to charitable work that could be considered responsible to the needs of society to some degree; much of the money collected by some groups has been shown to be used primarily for the support of the leadership of the religion. However, the appeal is made to potential recruits who have keen desires to do something worthwhile with their lives, especially activities that will have eternal values or will help people. There is a paradox inherent in this. The family that has raised a child to be concerned for others and to search for a deep meaning to life has also raised a child who could prove quite receptive, under the most ideal conditions, to the invitation of a cult group.

CULTS TEACH RELIGION, PRAYER, AND SCRIPTURES

Cult groups, once they begin to reveal their religious foundations, are quick to offer training or experiences that have the appearance of adding to the individual's spiritual life. While most cults require some form of financial commitment from people before sharing their deep teachings, the fact remains that cults do attempt to indoctrinate the inductee into the traditions, theology, and scriptures of the group. Many cults also place a high value on devotional life, offering frequent settings for worship and meditation, as well as teaching. Once a person has made the initial commitment, religious cults are not apologetic for their feelings about God, whether the Triune God of Christianity or their own concept of divinity.

THE ELEMENT OF FEAR

Fear is one of the most useful tools that any religion has to bring its followers into obedience or agreement; there is always just enough apprehension about the divine wrath of God or the influence of the devil to bring some people into line. The cults have mastered this technique completely.

Some groups simply bring followers to the point of believing that the devil is evil (which is true) and that all the world outside of the cult is evil, and therefore the devil's territory (which Christianity holds is untrue). Even more insidious are the groups that pursue former members with threats of eternal damnation or possession by the devil. Several groups are known for this technique, even though their leadership officially forbids such activity. One young woman, a follower of such a group for four years, was finally able to free herself emotionally from her apparent need for the cult and was living, both comfortably and happily, at home with her parents. One short telephone call changed all that. A cult member reached the girl in the middle of the night and issued a frightening warning. If the former member would not return to her group, her brother would be attacked by Satan. The brother had just suffered a serious fire in his home, so the girl was able to make an easy, albeit erroneous, cause-and-effect connection between the fire and the telephoned threat.[12] Another young woman, three thousand miles removed and two years later, experienced a similar call from another member of the same group. "If you don't come back with us, the devil is going to get you because he is out there in the world."[13] This woman was lucky, or so she feels; she had undergone a total withdrawal from the harmful effects of her former religion and was able to resist the threat, both through her own inner resources and by contact with several people who were able to help her maintain her perspective.

One of the best examples of the double-talk used by some cults was offered several years ago by one of the first victims of a cult to be rescued by his parents, a young man whose parents had to search the French countryside to find their son, who was recruited on the campus of an upstate New York university.

An element of fear is used to bind the members of the cult. Members are taught that their group is God's chosen people and insinuate that God's wrath might strike them down if they leave. . . . [but] they are told that they can leave anytime they wish, the idea expressed suggesting that the group is good and that they will not hold anyone against their will. The members are so psychologically dependent on the group by the time they hear this, however, that their chances of leaving are slim.[14]

We must recall that what we hope to gain is a general understanding of the entire cult phenomenon; not every cult uses the same (or even similar) recruiting techniques in a malicious manner. Not every religious cult teaches prayer and scripture; some make no pretense of offering opportunities for service, while others do have members performing what the group, and perhaps even society, might consider useful service, such as working with people in prisons or hospitals. Furthermore, we must remember that the cults are doing some things for their members that organized religions should be doing for their own followers, such as teaching prayer and scriptures, while also offering substantive opportunities for service.

DECEPTION

There is one other area of recruitment techniques that is used to some degree by almost every cult: deception. While it is almost redundant to repeat a theme that appears so often in other places, the fact remains that deception does occur, and it does not always emerge out of the well-intentioned enthusiasm of eager members who vigorously believe all that they say in street recruiting or Bible studies:

I was told to lie to those people we are trying to enlist or those from whom we tried to raise funds. I was told that I shouldn't every say that we were with our group or connected with [our leader]. Any possible means for getting money or people was justified on the grounds that the whole world outside was evil and Satanic. . . .[15]

chapter 5

Reactions of Parents

Almost every week the mailman delivers to people concerned about the involvement of youth in cults "wanted" posters from parents who are attempting to locate children whom they fear are lost in a religious cult. The picture is a handsome shot of a striking young man, a clean-cut, all-American type who was "last seen in San Francisco visiting friends of the family" or "disappeared from college campus without informing anyone of his destination." Have this child and hundreds like him disappeared into the carnival of souls, or is their disappearance and accompanying silence an indication of youthful escapism or rebellion—or perhaps even something worse? Whatever the causes for the absence, the anxiety of the concerned parents for the welfare of their children is obvious from the circulars distributed.

Parents are confronted by perhaps the most difficult decision of their lives when they discover a child has joined a religious cult. They often look back over the past fifteen or more years and feel that they tried hard to raise their child well, with love, support, understanding, and moral and religious guidance offered at every important moment of life. But then it happens; a person who has been a vital part of the family's love and future disassociates himself in favor of a "new family," surrounding himself with new friends, new authority figures, new beliefs about God, and new value systems.

Some parents react calmly by accepting the change in attitudes, behavior, and belief as a positive step for their children. In fact, in some instances such "conversions" are indeed positive; it is not uncommon for some groups to be effective in modifying unacceptable, or even antisocial, behavior and replacing it with more acceptable traits. Some people, for example, have been able to grasp hold of a cult religion and thereby escape differing forms of drug addiction. However, such behavior modification does not necessarily imply that a new religion is therefore a desirable adjunct to society, particularly if the behavior modification has been inflicted on the member by a means not necessarily preceded by some degree of informed consent on the part of the recruit. Furthermore, the fact that a group offers anything positive does not make the group itself a positive force necessarily; other factors must be taken into consideration. While the discipline required by the Armed Forces during the Vietnam conflict helped some people change their lives for the better, this observation cannot be taken to mean that all discipline in the army is beneficial to everyone; or that the Vietnam conflict could thereby be justified somehow as beneficial to society, based on that sole factor! For those who may need a rigid, authoritarian system of living, the cult experience might have some positive aspects, but these can be measured only by the extent of the problems these people possessed when they entered the group.

There are some parents who can accept cult membership because they feel that any group representing itself as dealing with God automatically must be worthwhile; this benign attitude of total acceptance of any religion is common in America. More than one swindle in the past has been grounded on the idea of starting a church or new religion!

Other parents will accept a child's membership in a cult because they fear that a total loss of communication may result if any differences or questions are aired. Of course, there are always a few parents who voice their approval of their children's religious activities who would also "approve" of almost anything that their children do, simply because these parents have chosen not to become deeply involved in the lives of their offspring.

Questions voiced by many parents reflect varying degrees of anxiety about their child's involvement. While many parents express some concern about the religious legitimacy of a group and their child's constitutional rights, there are other parents whose solicitude is rooted totally in secular views of man and society. These parents, both sophisticated and nonreligious, view it wrong for anyone, particularly a young person, to be so concerned about God and religion at a stage in their development when they should be studying and working with an eye to establishing a productive and mature life.[1]

Whether their concern is based on religious, psychological, or legal foundations, the parents who do have questions and concerns about cult affiliations have discovered that the most effective way to deal with such a massive maze of bewilderment, frustration, and anger is through group support. Several groups, whose membership rolls include parents, concerned clergy, psychologists, and lawyers, have been formed around the country in the past five years. Their primary efforts have been directed toward education of the general public through conferences and programs offered to schools and community groups, lobbying efforts in legislative forums, and the emotional support provided for one another.

Support of other parents' emotional needs is probably the most important function these groups can perform. Where else can distraught or confused parents turn at one of the loneliest moments of their lives, when their child calls and joyfully announces, "Hi, mom. Guess what? I've just joined . . ." There is little support to be found from groups that claim to attempt to bring together family members. Their boards and staffs are composed almost totally of members of either the very groups the parents distrust, or of their legal representatives.[2] Most clergy are ignorant of the problems that cults present, or the extent of those problems; their efforts to help are often limited to bland reassurances, such as "This is only another part of 'growing up,' which will soon pass." Some of the parents have been sued by their own children or by the cults themselves on charges such as kidnapping. Court costs to these families often run as high as a hundred thousand dollars to provide a defense against the lawsuits brought about by their "loving children" and encouraged by the cults that claim to "seek to reunite families."

Parents go through many of the traditional stages of grief that people must endure when a loved one dies. Even though actual physical death has not occurred, the sense of total loss can be just as great as in phyical death. Support groups of articulate and concerned parents and counselors are a great source of strength and direction at such times. Self-incrimination is a serious problem; parents are filled with a sense of guilt that may be totally unfounded. There is *no way* that parents who have made good use of all their God-given available resources and gifts could hold themselves responsible for a child's recruitment into a cult when that child is "love bombed" by an aggressive group on his college campus at a time when he needs new friends! Parents who have previously worked through their guilt feelings and have accepted the relative lack of their own complicity in their child's involvement are able to lend immeasurable help to others who are only entering the first stages of the guilt process.

It is not uncommon for most parents to grow highly frustrated during this family difficulty; understanding and answers to questions are not always as readily available as the situation might demand. And it is quite possible for that frustration to grow into a deeply rooted anger expressed toward the cult for the alleged wrongs parents sense their child enduring, perhaps needlessly. But support groups that are dedicated to providing parental encouragement and advice afford a potentially healthy forum for airing feelings. Even more important is the ability of parents who have been through contacts with cult religions to help prevent other parents from turning all their anger and frustration into unbridled hatred of those in the cult, whether they are leaders or rank-and-file members. There is a delicate balance between righteous indignation and the poisonous hatred that blurs the issues involved and often leads to drastic actions and hastily considered solutions. The people whom some parents consider "monsters" may indeed have duped their children, but to allow anger to evolve into hatred will not help the problem at hand come to a satisfying solution. While it is difficult to avoid the passions of hatred when your own children are believed to be hurt, all effort should be made to avoid that passion. Hatred can develop into even more serious problems, including a radical alteration of personality.

There is another image of parents concerned about their children that some of the cults, or the groups that actively support them, have put forth; some news media have tended to accept such assessments (which are not necessarily accurate or objective at all) with a great flourish of publicity. Parents, their friends, relatives, and neighbors have been subjected to assaults on their integrity, often because they simply dare to raise legitimate questions about their children's involvements in new religious groups. As we have already noted, there are always exceptions to every generalization, and the same holds true with parents; while most parents have acted either out of their own best interests or the best interests of their children, the symptoms of the cancerous hatred mentioned above have emerged in a few concerned parents. A very few parents have been driven to pursue their children for years after all legal means of recovery had been exhausted, and most illegal means as well; even court orders, designed to keep parents away from their children simply because the parents do not approve of their child's activities, are ignored. Whether such behavior has ever proved helpful in restoring either parent-child relationships or in insuring the well-being of the child is questionable. Happily, these parents are the extreme exception.

But the cults have grabbed onto the example of these extremist parents to make the blanket accusation that any parent who dares to question a cult is therefore an "abomination to motherhood,"[3] or that parental groups exist only as "vigilante" groups, which are out to quash all new or slightly different expressions of religion.[4] Such people undoubtedly do exist, if the law of averages is valid in this particular instance; but to condemn all parents and parental groups on the basis of a few radical examples is akin to condemning all new religious traditions and experiences *ipso facto* only because one or two such expressions are harmful. Is it possible, though, for a parent to remain totally emotionless when he discovers his child in a cult? Some parents can, but perhaps only because they have already emotionally disowned their child. But for the parents who are upset, emotional detachment seems impossible. One leader of a parents' organization acknowledges the problems inherent in this situation and issues a valid appeal to all parents of cult members: "I'm not saying that parents do not have the right to be emotional in this situation, [for] it is a highly emotional issue. However, in presenting ourselves to the public it is very important that we do not live up to the image of parents' groups provided by the cults themselves—that of vigilante groups, with little concern for facts and totally wrapped up in emotionalism."[5]

The best way to gain some insight into the tensions that

parents and family members often must bear may be to examine some of the experiences of a typical American middle-
class family whose son joined one of the nation's major and
best-known religious cults. The family's roots are in a major
eastern city, and their religious tradition is firmly rooted in
the Roman Catholic Church.

Sam and Lindy are hardworking, loving parents who have
been faithful to God through their active participation in their
church for many years; their children were also active in the
church, receiving many awards and taking part in many opportunities to serve. Everything about the family seemed as
normal as "baseball and apple pie," until one day when their
son, Tony, answered an advertisement in the local newspaper:

OPPORTUNITY TO SERVE MANKIND OFFERED TO
PEOPLE WHO LOVE JESUS. CALL [number given]

There could be no doubt about it; Tony's love for God was
very real. He had enjoyed an active prayer life and engaged
in regular works of charity. He appeared psychologically normal, although his parents considered him at the time of his
enlistment as "quiet and sensitive." The parents' anguish
and concern shows as they relate their experience, which had
not ended in 1978, four years later:

> When Tony left home to join the Group in answer to a
> help-wanted ad in the local newspaper, we were devas-
> tated, but we had no ammunition to fight his entry into
> the cult (which is one of the best known in the nation).
> We knew instinctively that it was wrong. We are Catho-
> lic and we are convinced that all our religious needs can
> be met by our own church. We began praying that his
> stay in this movement would be temporary, we hoped
> just a lark for him.
> After a couple of very trying visits home, during

which we were completely unable to communicate with him, we decided and were advised by our son's doctor as well as a priest whom we had persuaded Tony to talk with on one occasion, that we had to help him to get his mind back by deprogramming. This was done after much prayer.

We are a family of moderate means, and my husband is a conservative and cautious man. It was entirely foreign to his nature as well as my own to borrow the ten thousand dollars needed for this project and to leave during the coldest winter during this century in our eleven-year-old automobile from Philadelphia. The large amount of money needed was not because of high fees charged by deprogrammers (as the cults allege). They (the deprogrammers) were very reasonable. Legal fees were high. Transportation for all of those involved, plus motel rooms for the people involved, and food and security and many long-distance phone calls were the factors which made the price so high.

We obtained a conservatorship in court, and with the aid of the police we were able to get Tony from the Group house where he was at the time. We thought that the deprogramming effort was a success, but I must admit at the time that we were uneasy about his extreme quiet. He had always been quiet. . . . and (we felt) it must have been a strain for him to have to go through deprogramming. He apparently managed to con the deprogrammers, and after about four weeks in a rehabilitation center in New England, he escaped one day and went back to the Group center in Providence.

The day we were given that news, I believe, was the saddest day of my life. If we had been told that there was a death in the family, it would have been much easier to bear. I am not trying to say that I wish that had happened instead. I'm only saying that it would have been easier on us (to understand). Society has a way of coping with death. People understand and know how to offer sympathy. The clergy knows how to minister unto those who lose their loved ones in death. Society does not know how to cope with cult problems. Clergymen don't know how to counsel nor in most cases do they understand the need for spiritual help to those who are afflicted by the loss of one they love to a cult. Many people who see you in anguish do not know the right things to say, and many made us feel worse with the remarks they made . . . such as ". . . It must be God's will." God's will that our son devote his life to serving an anti-Christ? No . . . and we also know that the boy is not happy.

Two months after he went back, during which time we were not aware of his whereabouts, the cult informed us that he was taken to a psychiatric hospital in Washington, D.C. They said that it was a public hospital and that we would probably want to have him moved because "it isn't a very good place." We immediately checked with our doctors here and with some other doctors in the East and obtained recommendations for a psychiatrist in Baltimore, who agreed to treat Tony provided he was willing to go with him. Our son signed himself into the hospital in Baltimore, and we made arrangements to see that the expense of this would be taken care of, and it was very costly.

We discovered a few days later through a reporter from a local newspaper that the reason our son was put into the psychiatric hospital from the Group's headquarters was that he was standing by an open eighteenth-story window and they were fearful that he intended to jump. He was hallucinating at the time. This information was not given to us by the Group member who phoned us, but we verified it by talking to the detective who was sent to talk him away from the window. It is impossible to describe the heaviness which had been felt in all of our hearts when we heard this news.

In the hospital we chose, Tony was free to leave any time he chose (because of state law), and Tony chose to leave and go back to the Group's center on the day that his younger brother was graduating from high school. My husband did not attend the graduation because he felt he wanted to stay by the phone for news from Baltimore. No one knew what had happened to him when he left, and the Group there lied to the doctor who was trying to locate him by telling him that they didn't know where Tony was. The doctor found him by scouring the downtown area of Baltimore the following day; he spied our boy on a street corner with some other Group members selling candy. The doctor then persuaded the Group to send Tony back to the hospital, explaining to them the seriousness of his illness.

After about three months in the hospital, the doctor wasn't ready to release him, but since Tony was growing restless, agreed to turn over his care to a local physician so that he could rejoin his family. Tony was functioning very well and asked his father to try to find employment for him. The doctor emphasized the importance of getting him started working immediately, both to keep him busy and hopefully occupied to the extent that he would stay home from the cult and also to give him the self-respect that comes from being responsible for your own support.

It was an unpleasant task to go to friends and acquaintances explaining the necessity of finding a job for our son immediately, but his father was successful and Tony was pleased with the news that he was a working man with an equipment company. It was a small firm, and the people were both kind and understanding. Tony seemed contented and even proud of himself in his new career.

Alas, though it was his first weekend home, he left and went with the Group members for a weekend in Detroit. We were on edge all the time he was gone, and immensely relieved when he did return home that Sunday night very late. Group members had come to visit him at work . . . and he had spent an hour or two on several occasions at their center. We didn't object openly to this because we hoped that his need for the Group would diminish in time and we did not want to upset his convalescence. The doctor had told us it would be unwise and useless to demand that he stay away from the cult. But after six weeks with us, he disappeared again, leaving a note that he had rejoined the Group.

His doctor in Baltimore had warned us that full-time membership in this organization was going to cause him to have to spend the rest of his life in an institution, but he ignored this advice. When we tried to find out the details of his leaving, the Group's director here simply told us that he didn't know anything about it. We knew that was a lie. Tony had talked to him on the phone the evening prior to his disappearance from home.

Since his return, we had spasmodic contact with Tony, by mail and by phone. We know that he isn't well. We are extremely concerned about his temporal and eternal welfare. The Group director (a new one) has told us that Tony is having counseling every week. We have no way of knowing whether it is competent professional help he is receiving or whether the counselor is another member of the Group. We have requested that the counselor write or call us so we can know something about the quality of the care he is getting, but we have received no response to this request yet.[6]

Sam and Lindy are still waiting for Tony to return to his former life, to his family, friends, and career plans. No one knows whether he will ever return. Hundreds of parents live a daily life of emotional anguish in the very same hell on earth that Sam and Lindy share. But Sam and Lindy are typical of many parents in another, more important way. They have been able to see some positive effects arise out of this nightmare.

Our feelings during these past four years have been [grounded in] hope and faith in God, and sometimes total despair. We have been angry, hostile, sympathetic, and desperate toward Tony. We feel most of the time that he is a victim of the Group's messiah, but we are victims, too. We feel that he had the chance that many Group members would like to have had to get out and turned it down, even though it was given to him with a substantial sacrifice on our part; but we can't be sure whether or not he is responsible for his actions since he joined the cult, even during the times he was with us.

We feel sure that all of us have benefited in some ways from the cult involvement of our Tony. We have learned a lot about what is really important and what is trivial. Our eyes have been opened to the pettiness we see around us, and while our children do have occasional resentment of the emotional drain this experience has been for their parents, their attitudes are generally generous in their own willingness to sacrifice if they can do anything for their brother.

We are not constantly obsessed by our dilemma, but we have periods such as the past month or so during which there have been several important family events . . . when it is almost impossible for us to get our minds off the fact that Tony should be here with the rest of the family.

If we knew that he was doing something worthwhile and that he was growing in ability, knowledge, and/or skill and that he was truly serving God, we could easily accept his absence. On the rare occasions when we do get a chance to speak with him, we find that we are "on guard" all the time and fearful that we may say the wrong thing and drive him further away instead of bringing him back. There are endless unanswered questions in our minds. . . . We want him to be free to live his own life and to serve God in the way that we know he is capable of doing. The present situation is like a millstone around our necks. . . .[7]

Sam and Lindy are lucky in many ways. They still have contact with Tony; not all families enjoy this. They have both managed to maintain their physical and emotional health, as well as their spiritual well-being, during this severe family crisis. Many families have seen strong and healthy parents reduced to physical or emotional cripples from the exhaustion and strain under which cult parents often live. These two parents and their other children are financially fortunate, because they have not been confronted with any legal problems, other than the initial conservatorship, which have resulted from their son's involvement with the Group. Their parental expertise has helped their other children keep their frustration, bitterness, and jealousy to a minimum. Unfortunately this has not been the case in some families, where other children have had to endure serious financial hardships and personal sacrifice, often emerging both angry and bitter because of that sacrifice. Perhaps, most of all, Sam and Lindy, and many like them, are fortunate because they have been able to take a trying situation and learn some positive, upbuilding lessons from it.

chapter 6

Former Members

Donna is an attractive woman, now twenty-five years old and a trained professional in a health-related vocation. Several years ago, her life was quite different because she had been drawn into one of the strange mutations that emerged from the Jesus Movement, a group whom we will call the "Christian Family." This "Family" is still headed today, almost ten years later, by an attractive couple to whom we will refer as "David" and "Linda."

Donna emerged from her cult experience to resume her life on its former path through the process of deprogramming, which will be explored later on. She considers herself to be extremely fortunate, because she escaped and was able to recycle her life. But others who joined when Donna did, and even earlier, are still entrenched in this group, which its former members decry as corrupt and akin to a "concentration camp."[1] After working for several months as an agricultural worker, one member reported returning almost three thousand dollars, his entire salary, to the Family. "We just turned it over to the older brothers, and they turned it, in turn, over to Linda and David, I guess. There were hundreds of us working in the fields at the time, so they were taking in an awful lot of money."[2]

Field workers were pushed to make a total effort for six

days of the week and then were returned to the Family's base camp for a Sunday service. "If we were lucky, it was our one chance during the week to get a shower. We had one shower for about two hundred males. . . . To get a shower you would wake yourself up at three or four o'clock in the morning. There was only cold water, never hot water. To make matters worse, their toilets were always backed up. There were two toilets for those two hundred males; one sink, two toilets, and one shower."[3]

Members who have escaped report that David and Linda enjoy a standard of living that stands in stark contrast to their followers. ". . . [David and Linda] themselves live in the lap of luxury—fashionable suits for David and glamorous white gowns for Linda. Transportation to and from their secluded mansion is provided only by Cadillacs and Lincoln Continentals. . . ."[4]

Not to be outdone by the secular world, David and Linda operate a high-class clothing store in a major southern city, even though their tax-free religious foundation took in one million twenty-nine thousand dollars in 1975, according to Internal Revenue Service records.[5] Encouraging visitors to this tourist mecca to visit at their clothing store and perhaps spend several thousand dollars for a new country-and-western outfit, David and Linda have installed billboards along the Interstate roads into this city, with larger-than-life replicas of themselves, clad in country-western garb, waving at the tourists and proclaiming their store as "where the stars shop."[6]

David and Linda have also surpassed many other evangelists and cult leaders with the stories of their personal lives before they entered the religion business. Both David and Linda have been married three times each, with all previous marriages ending in divorce. And David has a police record; he served three months for receiving and concealing stolen property and was also fined five hundred dollars and served one year's probation for mail fraud.[7]

Donna's story of the David and Linda Christian Family is not always a pretty tale; no story that tells the truth about what some groups do under the guise of religion is pleasant to ponder. But Donna lived around David and Linda for almost three years, and her insights and experiences into the Family are typical of many reports that have been given by former members of this religion, which has altered the lives of several thousand young adults in its ten-year existence.

In the beginning, the David and Linda Christian Family *appeared* to follow the ways and mores of the "Jesus Freak" youth movement. David's six-page testimony tract, passed out by followers on the streets of Los Angeles and Hollywood, tells the Family's "supernatural" beginnings. Linda rarely gave her testimony. The first and last time I heard her life story happened in 1974 while she filmed a television program. Followers add more details to the Pastors' stories by telling about their lives under David and Linda's direction, progressing from 1969 to 1973 at the dope den (first church), to a two-story house (second church), to a former movie-star retreat, (and then) to the third church.

After I came in June 1973, several renovated "foundations" purchased by David and Linda housed families, brothers, and sisters. The housing conditions gradually became less crowded and more modern as followers, under David and Linda's supervision, remodeled and redecorated rundown buildings, including motel units, small houses, a bar, and two apartment buildings, and a Hollywood mansion.

The ideology and image of the group gradually changed with the foundations. On David and Linda's decrees, the jean-clad hippies crying "Repent or perish!" or "The world is coming to an end!" straightened up to appear clean-cut, and speak out against anyone who comes against the Christian Family with accusations, investigations, expositions, or attempts to deprogram followers. The local targets included a deprogrammer, a state senator, Jan (Linda's daughter and an exposer of the cult), and ex-followers or parents who testify about the misuse of followers and the deceit of the Pastors.

When Linda decided street encounters became too dangerous for followers to continue, the mailing of three antideprogramming tracts hit the churches of major U.S. cities, governmental agencies including the F.B.I. and C.I.A., as well as police departments, Chambers of Commerce, Rotary Clubs, Full Gospel Business Men's chapters, etc. In some cities, such as San Diego, California, Tulsa, Oklahoma, Joplin, Missouri, and Alma-Dyer, Arkansas, the residents listed in phone books received the same three tracts. I participated both in street witnessing and in the mailing efforts. In all cases, the interpretations, "facts," and answers came down from Linda to followers who repeated verbatum "the truth" to the public.

Now that I am apart from the group and allowed to see the other side of the story, the deceit of the Pastors becomes apparent. For example, Linda's "facts" related only part of the truth, inaccessible to isolated followers. She taught followers never to be put on the defensive. Her statements on television and to followers clearly show her attempts to discredit and name-call all opponents of cults. She professed to fight for the First Amendment and America's freedoms, while at the same time using the privileges of a nonprofit organization for personal gain and denying followers freedom of thought and action. She further deceived followers by saying all were "shareholders" in the California corporation (the church). But, in reality, the only share followers had was to work for, live in, and maintain David and Linda's Christian Family. Thus, David and Linda controlled followers' belief, attitudes, and actions to manipulate the congregation to witness for the Family testimony, and work for David and Linda behind the front of American idealism, God, and truth (the Bible), which was distorted for personal gain.

My involvement with the Christian Family began in June 1973 and ended in March 1975. My first evening in contact with the church followers concluded with my being "saved" and led to my total commitment several days later to "serve God" at the Family. Throughout my stay at the Family, I learned the following persuasive statements used on people who came to Family services. Initially, visitors speak to "guest talkers," who are trained Family members capable of telling guests "the truth." Persuasions and pressures to salvation include relating scriptures on compelling themes of repent or perish, end-time signs, fear of God, the wrath of God, the blood of Jesus, the sinfulness of man, uncertainty in life, and the end of the world. Besides talking about the "King James" Bible and the Family, guest talkers accompany the visitor to services, to dinner after services, to the prayer room, to the bathroom, and back to Hollywood or Los Angeles in the Family's guest vehicles. This constant attention influences visitors to make a decision and commitment for truth or consequences of physical and spiritual death.

Few newcomers resist and turn away from "the truth" presented at the Family. Most agree with the climaxing entreaties of the guest overseers at the altar call and follow them forward to kneel before the pulpit, professing their belief and agreement with Family persuasions by repeating the "sinner's prayer." Immediately after receiving this gift of salvation, the offer of receiving another gift, the Baptism of the Holy Spirit, draws the new convert into the prayer room. Over and over, the convert repeats "Praise you, Jesus, thank you, Jesus!" with the guest overseer and others joining in the prayer. The pattern changes only with increasing velocity and volume to a cresending, rapid-fire frenzy, which continues until the lead prayer breaks off and builds up again until the convert tires and either quits or speaks in "tongues." This whole process may last several hours.

The "Spirit-baptized" person then leaves the prayer room with the overseer to eat dinner and listen to reasons why they (new converts) need to come back to receive more teachings and to serve God. These reasons include biblical and Family examples, requirements, commands, and promises. These absolute persuasions entice or pressure converts to make a choice to "serve God" at the Family or "mammon" in the world. In any case, the decision to "walk with God" rests on the new convert, who encounters the alternative of losing the newly received salvation and falling back into the ways of the world, sin, and Satan. The saying "To ask is not the reason why, the reason is to do or die" could well apply to the Family's persuasions for salvation and commitment. According to the Pastors and followers, any questioning of Family beliefs borders on doubting God, disbelief, and blaspheming the Holy Spirit.

Those who, out of blind trust or fear, choose to return and join the ranks as baby Christians encounter many outward evidences of fundamental church functions. These forms include water baptism by immersion, Spirit baptism, communion, witnessing, prayer meetings, acknowledgement of spiritual birthdays, worship services, footwashing, and infant dedications. Except for mandatory daily Bible and prayer hours, all functions took place only when David and Linda arranged, announced, and/or officiated at each function. When David and Linda moved East from Los Angeles in 1974, every one of the functions, except services, prayer meetings, witnessing, and individual Bible readings and prayer hours ceased. Prayer meetings continued, being scheduled by David and led by brother overseers in his absence. Special prayer meetings were called by David to pray for Linda's healing from terminal cancer, for finances, for revival, and against the devil or anyone investigating, exposing, or suing the organization. Likewise, nightly services were led by brother overseers instead of David. Sermons were preached on salvation by older brothers and overseers instead of Linda. Individual, group, and assigned congregational Bible reading continued. Each follower had to take one daily prayer hour and one Bible hour or backslide and fall. Phone calls and tapes brought special messages from David and Linda to the followers in California, who had not seen the Pastors for months or years.

Followers believed at first that David and Linda would return to California. After almost six months of the Pastors' absence, followers changed and believed they would all eventually move to Arkansas and reunite with

God's chosen couple, who claim to have "started the Jesus Movement" and founded "the church to spark off the greatest world revival since Jesus Christ walked the face of the earth."

Followers, who decided to "forsake all" and to "take up the cross" to follow Jesus at the Family, ended up following the leaders who manipulated converts' lives like pawns on a chessboard. Actually, Linda led David and the entire flock. Followers regarded her as God's chosen handmaiden. They admired her professional sacrifice, courage, integrity, and wisdom. Followers characterized Linda as Moses the prophet, Paul the Apostle, or one of the two witnesses. Likewise David, held in equally high regard and worthy of double honor, guided the flock along with Linda. Both Pastors played the role as "spiritual parents" and formed in followers' minds images of supernatural ability, strength, wisdom, spirituality, and infallibility.

Members of the Family strive to attain and imitate the attitudes and examples set by these spiritual models. Followers trust and believe "beyond any shadow of a doubt" the "facts" and "God-revealed" interpretations and visions relayed over the pulpit, tape, phone, and television from the "chosen" Jewish Pastors. Followers, taught to "fear God," do not question or disobey the dictates of the Pastors. Thus, indoctrinated, dedicated, disciplined followers conform to become reproductions of the spiritual parents imagery. These subjects, with patterned minds and actions, can believe and be used by the Pastors, who control all with fear and guilt.

To aid in conforming converts to the Family, a mandatory indoctrination of three months "roots and grounds" all followers. During this time, a "baby Christian" totally submits to the tutoring of "older Christians," who watch and teach the babies, urging them to "receive" all from God and "resist" all from the devil. The Family then becomes the source of truth and the world outside the Family becomes the stronghold of Satan.

Gradually, the Family alienates and replaces family and friends in "the world" with new "brothers and sis-

During her stay at the Family, she was ill with bad colds and sore throats many times but never received any medical aid; they were told the Lord would make them better. . . . They lived in squalid conditions. They slept on the floor in sleeping bags, shared a bathroom with many others; the conditions were unsanitary but this was all done in the name of the "Lord." They were taught that everything away from the Family was the outside world, that it was an awful place . . . and that the only ones left (at the end of the world) would be those at the Family.

Before my daughter left the Family, she fasted for three days and claimed she flipped out because of it and was in a bad mental state and could not sleep. She was half out of her mind and noisy, and one of the elders came in and beat her up. They reported her to "David" who told them to get her out of there. They took her, bag and baggage, and dumped her at Hollywood and Vine at eight o'clock in the morning without a dime to call her parents. . . . We had to get help, so we took her to a hospital. She spent about three months in a state hospital. . . . It has been a long struggle for her and all of us, but today she is again a young, normal individual.[9]

One other person deserves the opportunity to share her experiences with the Christian Family. Her name is "Janet" and she was a member of the Family from its inception in 1968 until about 1973. While much of what Janet shared with the California State Commission in 1974 served merely to support the testimony of other speakers, her statements bear an even greater significance. Janet is both Linda's daughter and David's stepdaughter.

Her separation from the Family was painful; not only did she have to abandon her husband to the group, but her own life was in danger. She testified that "my life has been threatened, my children's lives have been threatened, I took a severe beating. . . . I lost all my property, and they have been trying to find me for three years." Her own sense of guilt about the life-style inflicted by her parents on hundreds of unsuspecting idealists brought her to the point of breaking her silence about the Group for the California hearing. "I must apologize to most of you parents whose children were involved in the Family because I'm as responsible, unfortunately, as my mother for having them stay there. I was also, in so many ways, a captive, so there wasn't a whole lot I could do about it. If you think it's difficult for your children to get out, think how difficult it was for me. My husband is still a member of the Family and has sent messages such as 'We are going to find you and bury you and your children alive. We are going to find where you are living and we are going to throw acid in your face. It is better that the children would be dead than to be living with a reprobate.' "[10]

One of Janet's primary concerns is that people join the Family thinking that they are starting to follow the teachings of Jesus Christ, when in fact she saw countless "converts" who were only "accepting my mother."

Linda and David's high life-style, with fine dinners in excellent Los Angeles restaurants while lesser members fed out of garbage cans behind these same first-class eateries, was one factor that convinced Janet that something was seriously wrong with this new religious group. But she was even more deeply troubled by the great amounts of money that came from television solicitations. Janet reported that the television shows featured shining young faces in neatly tailored clothing who would offer their "testimonies" of escape from drug addiction through the Family and its Pastors. "This television show goes on the air Saturday nights and Sunday mornings, and it all looks so clean and nice to those people sitting in Wisconsin, who say, 'Isn't it wonderful! They are getting these junkies off of drugs.' Let me tell you this: In the time I was there, I never met one kid who ever took heroin in his life. The biggest thing he had ever gotten into was marijuana or pills out of his mother's cupboard. And that's the truth. But now we see the same kid on the [television] show and he says, 'I was a junkie in Wisconsin, and I was dying, and my parents hated me.' These parents go to this place on their hands and knees, begging to see if their children are all right. . . ."[11]

Medication was frequently denied at the Family, and prenatal care was nonexistent. Janet recalled one young man whose cause of death was a brain tumor, but "it was operable and it was caused by malnutrition, colitis, and dysentery. This boy went hungry. I knew this boy, and . . . unfortunately I was one of the lousy people who caused him to stay. And now he is dead."[12] While Janet's observation that colitis, dysentery, and malnutrition caused the brain tumor may not be medically accurate, that is not the significance of this report. Rather, why didn't the Pastors or overseers encourage the man to seek surgical help for his tumor? Or, even more basically, why didn't the overseers see to it that this person received some medical attention for his colitis and dysentery? Even more convincing is Janet's allegation that this person suffered from malnutrition.

But Janet reports that other medical problems were common because members were not allowed to see doctors or to take medication. "You are not allowed to go to the doctor, yet my mother, at one particular time of the month, lay flat on her back . . . screaming 'I can't stand it anymore.' But these kids are not allowed to go to a hospital—some of them with a 104° or 105° temperature. I've seen this. I've lived there. I saw this happen. I have seen babies who needed medication who were not allowed to have this medication, because no medication is allowed on the premises."[13]

The Christian Family still exists and still poses a threat to young people. So many of the characteristics that numerous new religions manifest are common to the Family: isolation of members from society and family, emphasis on the devil-orientation of all outside the group, poor care and inadequate facilities, degradation of a person's concept of self-worth, the financial benefits given to the leadership, the financial manipulation of the membership, and the desperate attempt to project a normal, healthy image to the general public, without which they might not survive, either financially or legally. But behind the veneer of people "saved" from something evil are serious allegations, which add up to a cutting edge in the group's concerns for survival. This particular group has surrounded itself with a cardboard fort, which cannot survive even a superficial examination by its former members.

Not everything alleged about the Family here may be totally accurate; each person has offered subjective observations about his or her personal experiences and what each observed personally of others. But there is enough common ground between the perspectives of people involved at different times and places to suggest that a closer observation of at least this one group's "protection" under the First Amendment might be considered. And if this group could be said to be typical of the entire phenomenon, perhaps there are other groups that should be put to close scrutiny; dozens of other cults could have been examined here in similar case histories. If these new groups have nothing to hide, they should not only be eager to be exonerated from any accusations thrown at them but also ready and willing to throw open the doors to their churches, temples, recruiting centers, and accountants' offices to any responsible person seeking to dispel particular allegations made by both parents and the cults themselves. But many of these groups rebel against criticism behind a barrage of defensive verbage or legal actions, which only serves to increase the concerns and suspicions of people on the outside who desire an objective look at the inner workings of a religious organization that concerns their personal lives or the lives of people whom they love and perhaps even are responsible for.

Are these groups trying to hide something that we have not yet discovered? Is there something more dangerous to cult religions than extreme religious views, radically different lifestyles, or even financial manipulation? Just what are these groups afraid will be discovered about them?

chapter 7

Dangers

In the introduction we remarked that a significant number of young adults is involved in a
wide variety of cult activities. Yet some people say that the
problem is a passing phenomenon that will eventually die
out. But will it? There are a variety of ways in which the cults
are affecting the Judaic-Christian traditions of our culture
and country, the well-being of more than a few members of
the next generation of leaders, and even the political fabric of
the United States.

One distinguished rabbi has taken several major cults to
task for their apparent dishonesty and manipulation of many
members of an entire generation. His verbal questioning of
one particular group prompted that organization's director of
public relations to reply at length to the Rabbi's concerns.
The cult spokesman's concern was that the rabbi attributed
"no validity or integrity to those people who decide to join.
. . . You don't allow for the possibility that responsible young
people are sensing a need in themselves *and* in the world and
are taking the responsibility to meet those needs. Such is
what constitutes healthy and mature behavior."[1]

The rabbi's answer spoke directly to the problem that the
cult leader chose to bypass. The problem is *not* whether or
not a few members of the group, or even a simple majority,

or orthodoxy, these groups must stand accused of the subtle distortion of orthodox meanings and implications to reach their desired ends of theological confusion. Some leaders have remarked on this semantic confusion, urging them to be careful to remember that they may say the same words but those words do not mean the same to followers of the teacher as they do to those of us outside the group. In using terms such as "blood of Christ" and "Holy Spirit," one leader warns that ". . . we must define our terms. Many people may be misled because while using the same language or words, we don't mean the same thing."[4]

Organizations of national and local importance, such as the National Council of Churches of Christ, have taken strong stands against one major cult, primarily because of its deviations from the widest possible spectrum of either liberal or conservative expressions of Christian orthodoxy. The National Council's Faith and Order Commission reported that this group's theology was a "legalistic theology of indemnity in which grace and forgiveness play little part. The central figures of providence fail even when they are not believed—a vicarious failure is certainly not central to Christian affirmation. That is, Christ failed because the Jews did not believe in him and put him to death. That is double indemnity indeed, and its penalties are continuing antisemitism and the requirement that another savior come to complete the salvation of Jesus Christ."[5]

Even a critical non-Christian observer of this organization would have to give careful consideration to this group's overall view of Jewish traditions. According to a prominent Jewish spokesman, "From Abraham until the present day, Jews are seen only as people, devoid and emptied of any genuine faith and spiritual qualities. 'The inner contents are corrupt' . . . Further, the Jews have lost God's 'heritage' and are still being 'punished' for many sins."[6]

The paradox is that most of these groups make some claim

chapter 7

Dangers

In the introduction we remarked that a significant number of young adults is involved in a wide variety of cult activities. Yet some people say that the problem is a passing phenomenon that will eventually die out. But will it? There are a variety of ways in which the cults are affecting the Judaic-Christian traditions of our culture and country, the well-being of more than a few members of the next generation of leaders, and even the political fabric of the United States.

One distinguished rabbi has taken several major cults to task for their apparent dishonesty and manipulation of many members of an entire generation. His verbal questioning of one particular group prompted that organization's director of public relations to reply at length to the Rabbi's concerns. The cult spokesman's concern was that the rabbi attributed "no validity or integrity to those people who decide to join. . . . You don't allow for the possibility that responsible young people are sensing a need in themselves *and* in the world and are taking the responsibility to meet those needs. Such is what constitutes healthy and mature behavior."[1]

The rabbi's answer spoke directly to the problem that the cult leader chose to bypass. The problem is *not* whether or not a few members of the group, or even a simple majority, are highly motivated and totally in charge of their mental and emotional faculties. There are others to be considered. What about the people who were recruited by this group through the deceptive means that have been extensively documented in the secular press?[2] What about the reporter for the *New York Daily News* who almost lost his professional objectivity? The rabbi concludes, "My question remains. What do they [cult members] do to meet those needs [of the world]? It seems to me that a movement that consists almost totally of attending lectures, raising money, purchasing property, and enlisting new members is somewhat deficient in facing the needs of the world. I search in vain for any programs of social welfare or social concern." Paradoxical as it is, the fact remains that this same organization the rabbi is concerned about in this exchange is one of the chief exponents of the gnostic world view, which portrays the world as evil and discourages its members from associating with the world: "You must separate yourself from your Satanic environment. . . . You have to cut off the environment of your physical parents, and even the fallen husband and wife relationships."[3] Does this group try to meet the needs of the world, as its spokesman suggests earlier in his letter, or are members to "separate [themselves] from [their] Satanic environment," as their messiah urges?

Sometimes the greatest deception that these groups exercise is the double-talk we just saw an example of. Spokesmen for this same group claim "We seek to unite the family," while the leader himself calls members to separate themselves from the family. To add to the apparent confusion, this group also shares in the responsibility for directing the affairs of organizations that purport to be concerned about bringing families together in an effort at "conciliatory dialogue."

In any event it is clear that such teachings and encouragements from this particular messiah miss one of the primary lessons of Christianity, although the groups claims to be

Christian. A Christian is called by God to be a light in the world; the only way to be such a light is to be *in* the world. God's further expectation and hope of Christians is that they not be *of* the world; Christian expectations are that believers can share life with the worst sinners, but they are not to share in those sins. The fear tactics that cults direct toward relationships that members might have with nonmembers suggests that cult leaders either do not understand this basic principle of the Christian message or really do not trust God enough to transform their members or to strengthen them against temptation.

But this barely scrapes the surface of the real dangers that reside in many of these new organizations, which allege themselves to be legitimate religions.

THEOLOGICAL DANGERS

Most cults center on the teachings of some leader, usually self-proclaimed, who sits in power either as a Messiah figure or a self-anointed individual claiming direct revelation from God. These individuals, who fancy themselves either as the returned Christ or a modern-day St. Paul, usually put forth doctrines that are distinctly heretical, even though their roots may be in Christian scripture. We have already seen how many cults rely on creating an atmosphere of fear or distrust through their gnostic view of the world as evil and themselves as good; this gnostic tendency is further reinforced in some groups by "secret revelations," which are given only to a few, perhaps those to whom God chooses to share the secrets with or the people who are able to come up with the money to, in effect, purchase the secrets of these revelations. The divinity of Jesus Christ is often assailed with claims that he was a failure or not even God; some groups deny outright the long-accepted and proclaimed divinity of Jesus, while still believing "Jesus is Lord." While many groups will use this phrase, and others like it, to give the aura of authenticity or orthodoxy, these groups must stand accused of the subtle distortion of orthodox meanings and implications to reach their desired ends of theological confusion. Some leaders have remarked on this semantic confusion, urging them to be careful to remember that they may say the same words but those words do not mean the same to followers of the teacher as they do to those of us outside the group. In using terms such as "blood of Christ" and "Holy Spirit," one leader warns that ". . . we must define our terms. Many people may be misled because while using the same language or words, we don't mean the same thing."[4]

Organizations of national and local importance, such as the National Council of Churches of Christ, have taken strong stands against one major cult, primarily because of its deviations from the widest possible spectrum of either liberal or conservative expressions of Christian orthodoxy. The National Council's Faith and Order Commission reported that this group's theology was a "legalistic theology of indemnity in which grace and forgiveness play little part. The central figures of providence fail even when they are not believed—a vicarious failure is certainly not central to Christian affirmation. That is, Christ failed because the Jews did not believe in him and put him to death. That is double indemnity indeed, and its penalties are continuing antisemitism and the requirement that another savior come to complete the salvation of Jesus Christ."[5]

Even a critical non-Christian observer of this organization would have to give careful consideration to this group's overall view of Jewish traditions. According to a prominent Jewish spokesman, "From Abraham until the present day, Jews are seen only as people, devoid and emptied of any genuine faith and spiritual qualities. 'The inner contents are corrupt' . . . . Further, the Jews have lost God's 'heritage' and are still being 'punished' for many sins."[6]

The paradox is that most of these groups make some claim

to be Christian; they read and study the Bible, they talk about Jesus, they say their prayers, they feel empowered by the Holy Spirit. But despite claims of service to the poor, needy, or afflicted, the fruits of these organizations are often far from good. The "Jesus" whom they offer bears an alien resemblance to the Jesus of the Gospels. In reality, most of these groups practice little or no charitable activity. Their fund-raising techniques are often illegal and designed to direct monies toward the organization's financial pyramid (with the spiritual leader always at the top of the pyramid). But, even more seriously, these groups have been alleged to manipulate the minds of young people who join up with them, causing serious psychological damage, broken families, and sometimes completely ruined lives.

PSYCHOLOGICAL AND PHYSICAL DANGERS

While many people are refusing to acknowledge that cults are undermining a large number of our population, the fact is that some of these organizations continue to use their well-documented techniques of brainwashing and hypnotism, and thereby continue to grow. The American public simply does not want to admit that its youth could be susceptible to such forms of persuasion and mind manipulation. But it does happen, and the cults are protected under the constitutional right of "freedom of religion." But is there real freedom of religion for the individual once he joins up?

When most people think of a person being brainwashed, they envision the sort of mental torture that many soldiers endured under prisoner of war conditions, which were documented by Robert Lifton in his classic study of psychological damage to soldiers who were prisoners of war in the Far East during the Korean conflict.[7] This image of cult brainwashing is not far from the truth. But do we Americans, as sophisticated members of western civilization, want to admit that an intelligent young person might be robbed of his power of independent thought and choice? More than one commentator has indicated that the parallels between the indoctrination methods of certain groups and the techniques employed by the Chinese Communists and North Koreans are far too close to pass over or excuse.[8]

The power which a cult can wield to influence a person has also been shown by the news media. While cults have had to bear the brunt of many such accusations and allegations, their response, typically, has been either to issue flat denials or to admit certain problems and to promise their immediate correction. If the cults were as quick to alter their techniques of producing conversions as they were at making promises to make revisions, perhaps the questions might already have been answered. However, repeated investigations have discovered that even the groups that make the greatest number of disclaimers about their conversion techniques or who profess to be changing methods are the slowest to effect these changes, including problems of deceptive recruiting, isolation, and psychological manipulation through the methods already outlined.[9]

Closely related to brainwashing's persuasive and manipulative techniques are the hypnotic practices employed by some cults through the creation of isolated social situations in which converts are cut off from their accustomed social or emotional supports. Once again, Americans have an image of hypnosis: a bearded man with beady eyes swinging a watch before the subject's eyes, saying "You are in my power." With the cults, the method for inducing hypnosis is different, but the overall effect can be about the same.

Americans want to believe that a person makes his religious preference and exercises that choice through the freedom of religion guaranteed by the Constitution, as well as the freedom of thought and association, which we cherish so much. But it is actually possible to have a *nonholy conver-*

sion when influenced by a powerful leader who is carefully trained.

Let us consider the remarks of two recognized authorities on hypnotism. First, Frederick L. Marcuse, in *Hypnotism: Fact and Fiction,* reports on a controlled scientific experiment in hypnotic control to induce a vocal, convinced atheist into a religious state.[10] After three sessions, the attempt was so successful that it had to be terminated for ethical reasons. The avowed atheist began to attend church and to profess a belief in God! While this is only one example, it does suggest that a person can experience a total reversal of religious belief, and, in fact, be made a "believer," quite apart from the working of God in the process.

Likewise, in Karlin and Abelson's *Persuasion,* psychologist James McConnel is reported to state that he has been able to produce both religious and political shifts in ideology or belief. He makes the claim that he can change any person's behavior from whatever it might be to any condition someone else desires. McConnel claims that he is able to turn a Christian into a Communist and vice versa, or any other radical change that is physically possible.[11]

Significant new research, which reinforces this concept of *nonholy conversion,* is offered by Conway and Siegelman in *Snapping: America's Epidemic of Sudden Personality Change.* Their concept is quite simple. Through a variety of outside influences, including strong personalities, social pressures from peers, and other emotional reinforcements (threats, music, etc.), a person can be brought to the "snapping" point where radical personality change occurs. Conway and Siegelman point their longest fingers at manipulative religious conversion techniques and also self-realization movements that seek to degrade the subject's personality, while also attempting to steer him to the point of "conversion" or "rebirth." In addition to the cults, the authors give more than adequate attention to certain meditation techniques and health-related problems that can arise, as well as to the manipulative techniques of some "evangelical" preachers.

One example considered is Marjoe Gortner, the retired boy evangelist, who was once billed as "The World's Youngest Ordained Minister." Now living a relatively quiet life in California, Gortner claims that the primary concern at one of his services was to bring the congregation to a high point at a certain time in the evening. "For Marjoe, who has seen it a million times, the divine moment of religious ecstasy has no magical quality at all. It is a simple matter of group frenzy, which has its counterpart in every crowd."

" 'It's the same as a rock-and-roll concert," he (Marjoe) asserted. 'You have an opening number with a strong entrance; then you go through a lot of the old standards, building up to your hit song at the end.' " [12]

While not offering a complete answer to the questions posed by the cults, Gortner's admission of crowd manipulation leaves open the possibility that a cult could easily perfect similar techniques.

There have been numerous instances reported in counseling sessions of the apparent ability of cult members to produce self-induced hypnotic trances to avoid confronting the counsel; "speaking-in-tongues" is considered by some counselors to be the means of inducing this trancelike state, but the cause and effect relationship has not yet been conclusively shown. A number of young people who apparently had been successfully rehabilitated from their cult associations have reentered their groups because of posthypnotic suggestion induced through a variety of means. Some have encountered former cult members quite accidentally and drifted back into the group, while others have discovered themselves to be the recipients of frequent reminders from the group that they have entered back "into the world" and therefore face the consequences of that action. Other people have rejoined a cult simply because they picked up and read the same translation of the Bible they were accustomed to in their cult experience, usually the Authorized or "King James Version" of 1611. Another alleged symptom of hypnotic control observed in some converts is a marked change in handwriting techniques from cursive writing to block printing, as well as radical changes in grammatical structures, most often toward simple constructions.[13]

The spectre is not a happy one. Thousands of people have lost their original goals in life and placed their minds under the control of a religious leader whose intent may only be personal fortune and fame, or perhaps even political power. The overall effect on young adults has been likened to flagrant or borderline schizophrenia; it is a dissolution of the convert's mind into a childlike ego state, which no longer thinks for itself.[14] Many people of both Jewish and Christian backgrounds can sense parallels between certain cults and the manipulation used to control the youth of Germany during the Nazi era.[15] There, and even today, the mind of the individual merely adopted the thoughts of the leader and of the group.

Comparisons of letters written by cult members both before and during their religious adventures have shown shifts not only in handwriting and sentence structure but also in thought patterns; in a number of instances, comparison of letters written before and after the expression of cult commitment has shown that the ability to deal with abstract realities occasionally has been lost, to be replaced solely by simple thought patterns that deal only with concrete realities.[16] Members often write simple letters that respond directly to their parents' letters, with few references to the activities in which they engage as cult members.

The return to childlike dependency is so strong in one major cult that members have been documented medically to have undergone hormonal changes while in the cults; these alterations were manifested in such noticeable characteristics as loss of beard and vocal changes. Once the inductee has been freed from the cult's influence, his earlier physiological state has usually been restored.[17]

Similar bodily changes have been noticed by female members of some groups who have seen their menstrual cycles shift from a regular pattern that falls within accepted norms to a sporadic, random rhythm, if indeed they have any menstrual cycle at all during their involvement.[18] But there are still other changes that some members have reported, including radical changes in complexion, usually from clean, clear skin to faces often festering with acne. These same members are usually well past the customary age for such outbreaks of skin infections.

Other physical problems that may arise have been seen in some of the case histories presented earlier, including, most dramatically of all, the problems that can arise from a lack of medication and poor nutrition.

SOCIOLOGICAL DANGERS

The most apparent and direct result of cult activity is the breakdown in family relationships. Cults characteristically draw their members off to be with other cult members. Occasionally, members are sent to cult training centers to be immersed in cult indoctrination and activity, or are sent to colleges or seminaries run by the cults themselves and devoted to fostering cult beliefs, peer group support and pressure, and financial control over members. Such practices remove the convert from familiar social and emotional supports that might promote either doubt or anxiety.

Once again, we come back to the fact that many cults use a common ploy of satanic influences in natural family life. "If you believe we are right, and your parents believe that we are wrong, then wouldn't you agree that your parents are under the influence of Satan?" Once the convert has subscribed himself to this line of thinking, the next step is to enjoin him to leave the influence of the devil.

Some cult groups are supporting a conversational approach to understanding between parents and cult members, which they call "conciliatory dialogue," while other cult leaders stress that they do not mean to cause the breakup of the natural family unit. One cult spokesman wrote to a member of the Jewish community that

> there have been instances, as you report, where because of an individual's own commitment to the [group], and his parent's opposition to it, estrangement has resulted. However, this is not at all our wish. The instances of estrangement to which you refer represent the exception rather than the rule. . . . What I say is true. In the great majority of cases, individuals who join our [group] come to feel closer to their parents and relate to them more maturely and lovingly than before. I suspect you have little or no evidence of this.[19]

Once again we are confronted with several different viewpoints being expressed about the philosophy or policies of this particular organization coming from its leadership. The public statements, clearly stated, announce concern for the unity of the family. However, the Messiah-leader of this group is the very same man whose remarks about natural parents being a part of the satanic environment we reported earlier. Whom are we to believe? The man who is appointed by the organization to be its mouthpiece or the statements of the leader himself?

As if that were not enough to cause concern, can we look beyond the apparent confusion of words and view the "loving" actions that this same group encourages toward parents who rebel against the group? A member of this group was interviewed on a national television show about the lawsuit he had recently filed against his parents. Their only "crime" was an effort to have their child deprogrammed against his will because they felt, to the best of their knowledge, that he had joined the group without giving informed consent to most of what had happened to him after joining. When asked if filing a $1.1 million suit against his parents was a loving thing to do, his response was all too characteristic of the phenomenon we seek to understand: "Of course, suing them is the loving thing to do." It was said with all apparent innocence and sincerity. Could it be that there is confusion at the highest levels of this well-polished group? Or is the basic truth that the group is grounded on deception, directed both toward its members and also the general public?

Some cults claim that the individual has the freedom to leave at any time and is allowed to pursue whatever course of education he desires. While some cults do "lock their doors" at night, others maintain some form of open-door policy that appeases the public. But there is no need on the cult's part to fear the open door once a person's mind has been successfully manipulated into a position supportive of the cult. While some do simply walk away, the percentage of loss through this sort of individual escape is small; there is little chance that converts will leave freely, and that chance decreases as the member remains longer and longer in the group.

Do the cults seek to brainwash their prospective members? Is there a serious threat to the fabric of the American family because of these new religions? Some might say "only time will tell," but the answer is already with us, in part through hundreds of broken families who have not seen or heard from children, whom they still love, for many months or years. On a nationally syndicated television program, a man admitted to using many classical brainwashing techniques, including sensory manipulation, lack of food and sleep, and peer pressure over prolonged periods of time to produce over five thousand converts to one cult over a five-year period. In spite of such a confession before a national audience, which required a great deal of humility and courage, the cult's principal lawyer, also a guest on the same show, would only reply over and over, "that simply is not true."[20]

POLITICAL DANGERS

The possible "doomsday effect" of the cults is obvious. It is not impossible that a cult leader with a megalomaniac personality could draw around him a group of people, submitted to his authority, who would go so far as to bear arms in the streets. One political activist, writing in a political newsletter that appears to support actively the goals of one particular new religion, wrote that the rifles in the street during the American Revolution will again be in the streets whenever "noncompliance and lawsuits" no longer suffice and the courts turn against the "cause."[21]

This statement was printed in a newsletter recommended to followers of a particular Bible teacher, whose adherents number over twenty-five thousand around the world. The leadership of this organization openly espouses a strong, fervent sense of patriotism. In fact, they believe that the Constitution should be "rightly divided," just as the Bible should be also. Of course, for the Scriptures to be "rightly divided," inspiration either comes from the leadership or must be approved by the leadership before being promulgated. This group has also been accused of "block voting" in communities where its membership represents a substantial proportion of the electorate, and also of unfairly influencing the outcome of state elections because of the aggressive campaign tactics of followers imported to assist with the elections.

Another well-known group has openly attempted to infiltrate the halls of government in Washington, D.C., through a strong lobbying effort, as well as through efforts to keep former President Nixon safe from impeachment proceedings, and attempts to place at least three cult members on the staff of every member of Congress. The cult's leader has been alleged to enjoy political connections with his homeland, its dictatorial ruler, and its well-organized intelligence operations. This group is extremely sensitive about the allegations made concerning its leader, whom they regard as the messiah. They have recently released a highly prejudiced viewpoint of the congressional hearings called to investigate covert foreign intelligence operations which proceeded slowly during 1978. The leader's translator and closest associate was called to appear before a congressional committee to answer questions about the alleged connections between the religious organization and the intelligence community. Rather than confront the issues raised by the committee in the hearings, the publication reports only the responses of their spokesman as absolute "truth," with no opportunity for cult members to examine other information presented to the committee. This attractive-looking piece of propaganda was also circulated widely through the American religious community as an authoritative statement.[22]

Is this group political or apolitical in nature? Its spokesman denies the charges of political interests, just as his counterpart denied allegations of the underlying desire to break up the nuclear family. But can we read the statements of this "religion's" messiah and still believe that there is *no possibility* that politics are not a significant part of this religion?[23]

When we are in our battle against the whole nation of the U.S.—whatever village, whatever town you may visit, you must have confidence; and with that zeal you can have the love of God and can be resolved to smash the whole world.

Democracy is more or less ideal, but it is a man-made theory which is doomed to perish.

The present U.N. must be annihilated by our power.

We must have an automatic theocracy to rule the world.

Democracy, Communism, and even religion have failed. We can only be scornful of past ideologies.

When man fell the first responsibility was on Eve. . . . In Korea the time will come to fight with arms. The time must come when the blessed wives must fight with the satanic world on the front line, actually with arms. Now we are fighting with Christian churches and later with the satanic nation.

chapter 8

Deprogramming and Rehabilitation

Getting Out: The Emotional Battle

The involvement of young adults in cult groups, whether religious or pseudoreligious in nature, raises profound ethical questions for both the medical and legal professions, as well as for theologians and family workers. The one word that the cults both fear and abhor is "deprogramming" because, when effectively used, the process of deprogramming is able to cut through the cult's usage of mind-control techniques and return a person to personal integrity. While the cults might be able to raise valid legal questions about both the legality and practices of a few deprogrammers, there is only one real reason that the cults could fear the concept of deprogramming: if a person can be *deprogrammed*, he must have been *programmed* in the first instance.

One legal expert has put his finger on why it is difficult to prove that a person has been initially programmed. Many cult organizations bring a person to the conversion (what some would call the "snapping") point through a progression of stages. While it might be argued that the inductee has given his consent to each separate stage of the overall process, such consent may have been obtained without any prior knowledge of the end effects. In other words, full consent might have been obtained over a period of time, but only through a series of seemingly (to the inductee) unrelated events.[1] The process resembles what happens when dirt gets into an automobile's gas line. First the filters should be checked, then the carburetor is cleaned. If the problem persists, the carburetor must then be overhauled. Finally, as a last resort, the entire fuel line must be drained and cleaned to remove the dirt. Each successive stage builds on the past and is directed toward the end results, although the consequences of those ends are not necessarily apparent at the beginning.

Former cult members assert, almost unanimously, that they can sense in retrospect the methods of mind manipulation that their groups used on them, as well as the personality changes they endured. These same members are often quick to give credit to the overall process of deprogramming, which they allege lifted them from their mental imprisonment and restored them, or so they feel, to their accustomed personalities. "Due to my participation in this cult, my personality changed completely. I lost my identity and was only what the cult wanted me to be—a smiling puppet. They taught me that God's work comes first, regardless of tests or schoolwork. They made me feel guilty if I did not attend fellowship. My grades dropped from Bs to failing marks, which were not representative of my previous academic achievement."[2]

Another member of this same group found that he also suffered from a manifestation of mind control. "One reaches the point where he believes in the integrity of the leader . . . and is no longer able to question his teachings. He destroys the individual's confidence in his ability to interpret the Bible with the guidance of the Holy Spirit. He is such a dynamic and persuasive leader. . . . The organization discourages associating or living with nonbelievers, including parents or friends that might cause one to develop negative thoughts or to doubt [the group]. . . . [the leader] encouraged us to try reading only [group] literature and the Bible for three months and assured us that we would be a changed person by doing this. . . . We were also discouraged from reading the news- papers or watching the news on TV or anything which would cause us to develop negative thoughts."[3]

There are basically two ways out of situations such as these. It is not impossible for some people who are character- istically strong willed and questioning to be able to rise up and walk away from a commitment to a religious cult. How- ever, the chances that such an escape through voluntary means might be successful, or even possible, decreases as the level of commitment or length of membership increases. Of course, it must also be allowed that *some* cult members may remain in a group totally of their own free will, with no hint of persuasive coercion. The American Civil Liberties Union sensed the tensions in this question several years ago. "It seems clear, then, that at least some members willingly stay in the cults and are not 'brainwashed' into staying. But do all of them willingly stay? The answer can only be a quali- fied yes."[4]

One person who willingly escaped from a major organiza- tion did so because he was able to recognize a broad picture of what was going on around him. "After a month of that in- sanity, I was able to escape on my own. It was entirely my decision. After I became aware of the evil nature of [the] or- ganization I could not morally stay. . . . I believe though . . . that many of the young people who go to these seminars . . . are put under such heavy coercion and mind manipula- tion that they are unable to leave on their own free will. . . . Their admirable ideas are being exploited by [the leader] and his henchmen for their own personal gain."[5]

For those who are not able to walk away, the only path available for regaining their former personalities appears to be deprogramming, a threatening word for what represents a new field in the mental health services. Currently the demand for this skill is tremendous, but the number of people qualified to administer this treatment therapy from both psychological and theological perspectives is sorely limited.

The basic concept behind deprogramming is simple, but the execution of that concept is an extremely delicate therapy, which must *not* be attempted by well-meaning but unqualified individuals. The basic problem is how to restore the individual's ability to think for himself. How can the deprogrammer bring a person to the point where he can make *another* decision about his new religion, and perhaps his first *informed* decision?

The overall process might best be called repersonalization.[6] The desired goals are to bring back old language skills and memories and to restore personal relationships, while at the same time trying to prevent relapse. Even more important is the effort *to restore the cult member's ability to make personal choices*, apart from the influence of the group or its members. Of course, it has to be recognized that such an opportunity to make a free and informed decision unhindered by any psychological manipulation or deception may result in the person deciding *for himself* to return to the group.

The cults accuse deprogrammers of "reverse brainwashing"; of course, this implies that the initial brainwashing does exist! Because deprogramming is such a new form of therapy and also is as vulnerable to quackery as any other healing art or spiritual teaching, there are, admittedly, bad deprogrammers. A few manipulators are out for the "fast buck" and prey on parents in their grief and confusion; after discovering that their child was in a cult, one distressed parent discovered himself pestered by such operators:

> The callers have remained anonymous but they have informed me that they would give me further information

if I agreed to meet with them. When I inquired as to what fee they charged for such service, I was given a figure of $1500.00 plus expenses that would probably come to a total of $5000.00. I further inquired as to the qualifications of these "deprogrammers" and they stated that they had people who had been members of [the same organization] and of similar organizations who were well prepared to deal with any situation which arose.[7]

However, this type of psychological buzzard, scavenging on the emotional injuries of confused parents, is by far the exception rather than the rule. Most ethical deprogrammers are so busy that they must turn away many more cases than they can help, rather than wasting time soliciting clients.

Another source of "bad" deprogramming arises from the well-intended efforts of some former cult members and other highly motivated individuals who lack either the psychological or theological expertise to accomplish any sort of positive repersonalization. Most of these people are driven to help others because of their own personal contacts with cult religions.

One other source of "bad" deprogramming is the person who assumes that all cults are alike in theology; however, even the most subtle distinctions in theology must be thoroughly understood to effectively promote renewed inquiry by the cult member of the group's theology. Some clergy fall into this theological trap by assuming that their own extensive knowlege of their faith's doctrine will be sufficient to help a person "see the light." While such an approach might prove successful, the real risk also exists that a deprogramming session could result in little more than a theological debate for which the cult member could prove much better equipped and conditioned than the clergyman. The eyes and the brain are close neighbors in the human head, with closely related functions; however, would you allow a neurosurgeon to perform a delicate cornea transplant? In the same manner, the fact that a group's theology might resemble Christianity and even be identical in some points is not by itself sufficient for any Christian to try deprogramming through theological debate alone.

Happily, though, there are very few people performing "bad" deprogrammings. The majority of deprogrammers are teams of qualified theologians and mental health professionals who willingly submit their work to peer evaluation.

It is not advisable to describe exactly what happens in a deprogramming session because cults have used such information in the past to program their people against deprogramming. However, the general process, usually with a mental health professional as well as a clergyman well versed in the particular cult's theology present, is to confront the individual with information about the group and questions about their beliefs and behavior, with the goal of helping the person regain his own ability to independently question beliefs and to consider the effects of cultic practices on himself. Former cult members, successfully deprogrammed themselves, can be of great assistance to good deprogramming because of the very precise questions and personal experiences they can share.

Some cults are quite open about their concerns that members might be deprogrammed, and they take precautions to insure that such efforts will prove unsuccessful. "The people at [the ranch] told us that deprogrammers would physically torture us to get us to change our minds."[8] Physical violence, however, is not a normal part of deprogramming, although some cults program their members to resort to violence in order to resist any such efforts directed at their person. Nor can the charge of "reverse brainwashing" be substantiated against ethical deprogramming. The classical tools of brainwashing (lack of sleep, reduced caloric input, sensory bombardment, the inability to ask questions, limited access to toilet facilities, and other means of personal degradation) are *not* used in responsible deprogramming, nor are they needed!

One cult member relates quite clearly his own thoughts during an aborted deprogramming:

> Since I could not deny what I knew was true, and since they [the deprogrammers] had no logical arguments to prove it false, I could keep that deep within myself as a rock-solid foundation on which I could keep my sanity and strong faith in God, in [the group], and in [the leader]. Following the biblical injunction not to "throw pearls before swine," I never argued with the teachings again, but I kept them secret within my heart.
>
> I was cooperating. . . . I had several good intellectual conversations [with one deprogrammer]. He seemed the only person there who was willing to talk openly with me as a person, though he disagreed with [the organization]. Everyone else there was acting in a way calculated to alter my beliefs, as if I were a puppet to be manipulated. The more I cooperated, the better my chances to escape. . . . After five days [of deprogramming] I agreed to go to [a rehabilitation center] where my imprisonment would be more lax and I could more easily get away.[9]

In a small pamphlet entitled *How to Survive Deprogramming,* one cult member has provided a number of tips on how to evade questioning, how to set demands, and how to trap your deprogrammers into legal mistakes, which later can be used in lawsuits.

> First of all, it's important to understand the rules of the "Game." If you realize that it is a test, then you will know that it can and must be passed. If you know in your heart that you are God's child, then ultimately He must claim you. In the meantime, you should use the rules to your advantage:
> 1. They don't dare hurt you very much. The deprogrammers are afraid of the law. . . .

2. They can't force you to talk. They'll want to engage you in argument, but they cannot physically force you to read, speak, or think about anything.

3. You don't have to believe what they say! They're convinced that they're right or at least they're too afraid to consider that they might be wrong. Much of what they say is trivial—yet they treat it as significant.

4. They can't deprive you of your basic necessities. If things start to get thick, there are many ways to break up the atmosphere; such as go to the bathroom; take a shower; brush your teeth; wash your face; do exercises; eat; drink; do such things as call your lawyer; see your parents, or read some other material. Don't be afraid of hurting their feelings, surprise them!

Make demands. Make unreasonable demands and then stick to them. I demanded a written guarantee that the conservatorship would not be extended. If all those things are demanded already, then demand equal time for study of [Scripture] and for prayer. Anything, then "no guarantee, no cooperation." Never let your position seem unreasonable. Then they'll accuse you. You can respond, "I'm perfectly willing to cooperate with this whole ridiculous brainwashing session, but not until I have some basic guarantees." Then accuse them of being unreasonable. DON'T COMPROMISE.

Of course, one of the paradoxes of this cult member's advice is the whole area of basic necessities. If "breaking up the atmosphere" is a goal of the cult member, what good would it do to ask for food, unless you seriously thought you had a chance to be given it? But this believer's group is one of the primary complainants who state that deprogrammers deprive their subjects of food. However, our expert on surviving deprogramming continues, and finally concludes:

Finally, you should try to have things physically your way as much as possible. I demanded to sleep on the floor (because beds gave me a bad back). I demanded that no one smoke in the room with me. I demanded that no one of the opposite sex sleep in the same room as me. I demanded privacy in the bathroom. I demanded that everyone clean up the room in the mornings, and that someone change the towels and take out the garbage. Also, it would be good to demand things like seeking a physician, etc., immediately. It would be a good chance to escape, and a good way to break up the monotony. Demand that parents be in the room at all times. Mine weren't, but recently it was a stipulation made in court. I always kept bugging them, "what about all the skiing and movies I heard about. Let's go out!" If you're clever, it can almost be fun. One deprogrammer was being really cute and asked me to sing her a song "please." I sang a really powerful song about the persecution of the early Christians and inside she got really angry. It was great. Try not to lose your humor. Some time or another, really challenge the deprogrammers one at a time, so that they'll take off their masks and show their true selves. They're not worried about you as an individual. They hate [the leader] and they hate [the organization]. And they are determined to destroy both. When you understand this in your heart, you will no longer be susceptible to any "niceness." One last thing. Make a mental note of all the rules they break, so as to press charges when you are free. You can tell them, "you'd better be careful, I'm taking you to court when this is over!" But if they're not, smack![10]

In spite of the accusations by the cults that deprogramming must not only be evil but also a source of violence, researchers interviewing former cult members who have been through responsible deprogramming and rehabilitation have found little, if any, evidence that would substantiate the charges levied by the cults. The most vocal opponents of deprogramming, because of its alleged violence, are people within the cults. But physical violence is not a normal part of deprogramming, nor can the charge of "reverse brainwashing" be substantiated against ethical deprogramming. Many former cult members have been openly thankful that their parents chose to have them deprogrammed; "my parents gave my life back to me" is a sentiment commonly expressed by former cult members about their deprogramming experience and its outcome.[11]

One of the major sources of "information" on the violence that is alleged to be involved in deprogramming is a booklet called *Deprogramming: Documenting the Issue,* produced in early 1977, according to its front cover, under the joint sponsorship of the American Civil Liberties Union and the Toronto School of Theology. The editor of this collection of affidavits and magazine reprints, as well as transcripts of spoken remarks, is a theologian with interesting dual credentials: he is a professor at the Toronto School of Theology and holds a similar academic position at the seminary of this country's most vocal and powerful cult. However, his institutional affiliation with the cult seminary is not once mentioned in the contents of the booklet, although it would seem to cast some doubt on the editor's ability to remain objective and fair to all sides of the issue. In fact, the contents of this booklet are lopsided; the "documentation" provided reflects only one side of the question, the cult's. The underlying presumption of the booklet is that the cults are protected under the First Amendment; there is no consideration given to the protection afforded to the individual members under that same amendment. Nor is there one single favorable statement about deprogramming from either professional counselors or former members, although such comments are readily available.

But the most damaging bit of information that the ACLU and the Toronto School of Theology have put forth in this booklet is the reproduction of a pamphlet called "Deprogramming: The Constructive Destruction of Belief; A Manual of Technique." Allegedly printed in England by two groups that claim to be concerned about cults, this manual purports to present basic techniques for deprogramming, including some of the classical brainwashing techniques including food termination, sleep withdrawal, shame-inducement through nudity, verbal stress, the "destruction of holy works" (i.e., the alleged destruction of cult artifacts), and sexual coercion. Actually, much of what they recommend for "good deprogramming" is little different from what reporters who have infiltrated some groups report back as their own experiences within the cults!

If this manual was a legitimate production of people who actually were involved in promoting deprogramming, then it would stand as sufficient reason to work for the banning of this type of coercion as much as the banning of any type of coercion inflicted by a religious cult. However, many observers feel that the manual is not a legitimate production but rather the combined effort of several cults, aimed at discrediting the work of deprogrammers. First of all, the "description" offered of deprogramming fits almost too closely the allegations levied by the cults themselves. Second, several of the groups listed as "active in countering the menace of the cults" in the back of the booklet have disavowed any association with, or even knowledge of, the people represented as putting forth this booklet. Finally, one American television producer, who has done several documentaries on cults, flew to London to track down the people who claimed responsibility for this manual and discovered that the alleged sponsoring group consisted of one individual, who refused to be interviewed.[12] Could it be that the "group" that sponsored this pamphlet is composed of members of the same group that, according to the Anglican bishop of Bristol, has been doing their house-to-house proselytizing and fund-raising by giving the fraudulent impression that they are working in cooperation with the (Anglican) Church of England?[13]

The American Civil Liberties Union suggests in its deprogramming documentation that all deprogrammers work through a network that is allegedly led by a former California social worker who specialized in youth work.[14] The charts provided to illustrate this allegation even suggest that this single individual has a controlling influence over several parents' groups scattered around the country. This allegation of a deprogrammers' network with a monochrome philosophy is more effective at scaring people ignorant about deprogramming than it is in relating any of the truth behind the phenomenon. There is no formal network or association of deprogrammers, although some deprogrammers do share information and insights with each other, just as lawyers for the ACLU probably do. But the ACLU's assumption that even parents' groups are involved in promoting deprogramming as a well-organized national effort counters both the written and verbally proclaimed desires and goals of the groups mentioned that they do not function, as a group, in deprogramming efforts; as with any organization, the group cannot necessarily be held accountable for the independent actions of its individual members. In fact, the idea that there is a common network of deprogrammers all influenced by "direct ideological influences or commonality of personnel"[15] can be disproven by talking with any five deprogrammers and noting the differences in techniques, discovering perhaps as many as five different approaches to both the psychology and theology involved.

Another allegation made in the ACLU manual, and supported by the cults, is that deprogrammers are making a fast dollar off the parents of their members. Whether the money involved is a "fast dollar" or not depends on how an observer would evaluate the overhead involved in a professionally competent deprogramming and rehabilitation. There are three factors that keep the costs of such assistance high. First is the length of time usually needed for rehabilitation, often four to six weeks, under the supervision of a qualified medical and psychological staff, as well as recreational and maintenance people, in a live-in situation offering abundant options in therapies and activities for those being helped. Second, legal costs related to this type of work are a significant factor in overhead. One deprogrammer has estimated that well over 50 percent of the fees he must charge are directed toward the legal expenses encountered in facilitating the battle against mind control. The third factor, as we saw in an earlier case study, is the peripheral expenses encountered in deprogramming, such as long-distance telephone calls, travel expenses, and lodging.

Without a doubt, reputable deprogramming is an expensive procedure in most instances, with the costs for both deprogramming and rehabilitation often running over five thousand dollars. But the ethical deprogrammers are *not* living in mansions in the countryside of upstate New York, flying around in private jets, or being served dinner by loyal followers. The expense of such rescue may be considerable, but deprogramming and rehabilitation are not "high-profit" lines of work.

Many people say that deprogramming is not necessary with cult members; however, the evidence points to the contrary. Parents have attempted to talk their children out of cults, almost always to no avail. Local pastors have often tried, and usually failed. Even the traditional psychiatric methods of treatment and therapy have not proven effective. According to Dr. John Clark, a psychiatrist at Harvard Medical School, who testified before the Vermont state legislature:

> . . . . while outer symptoms resemble flagrant and classical schizophrenia, the mental state does not respond to antipsychotic drugs or accustomed treatment, such that normal techniques can't restore thinking processes because physical control can't be exerted for long enough to use confrontation therapies.[16]

What the cults really object to is the fact that deprogramming assists an individual "to step out and take an objective look at what you have put your life into."[17] In addition, it seeks to shift the cult member's personality back to its original state, the process of *repersonalization*. With some individuals, the process requires several days of constant attention, while with others only a few moments might be required. The difference in time comes both from the depth of involvement in the group and the skill (or sometimes the luck) of the deprogrammer in discovering the key that will bring about an objective perspective in the cult member. Once the break is made in the individual's thinking processes to restore free thought, there is a fairly rapid return to the mental and intellectual state that the cult member possessed before his indoctrination.

Is deprogramming a useful and helpful tool to legitimately give a cult member another chance to make his commitment, or is it, as the cults allege, a perverted form of mind control and "brainwashing"? One religious group, which has been most concerned about the presence of freedom of religion in religious cults, is the Jewish community; some of America's outstanding civil libertarians are Jewish and have been supporters of groups such as the American Civil Liberties Union. However, the voices of many in the Jewish community are echoed in the statement adopted by the Union of American Hebrew Congregations' Biennial Meeting in November 1977:

> While the right to proselytize in our society is protected by constitutional guarantees of religious liberty, we are concerned, nonetheless, by the current intensification of missionary activity directed towards Jews—in many parts of this country. Those guarantees neither legitimize nor justify tactics which some missionary groups and cults use . . . coercion, misrepresentation of the meaning of religious symbols, abuse of religious rites and practices. This deception often violates the civil rights of those members who are its victims. Membership in some cults is frequently sustained by tactics of physical and emotional coercion which represent a

violation of civil liberties; specifically, freedom of choice and freedom of religion.

We affirm the right to use legal deprogramming efforts. We fully understand the motivations of and empathize with Jewish families who may have lost a child . . . to a cult, but we cannot affirm the right of the use of illegal deprogramming efforts which use illegal coercive measures, even when they are designed to return an offspring to the family faith.

The book of Proverbs teaches "train a child in the way he should go and even when he is old he will not depart from it" (Proverbs 22:6). It is an admonition worth our serious effort.[18]

One point in the above resolution is worth stressing. Jewish leaders are concerned about a decrease not only in the level of practicing faith amongst the Jewish people but also in the decrease of the total number of Jews in this country and in the world. However, they are unequivocally against illegal deprogramming, even if their avoidance of such efforts might mean that a child would never return to the "family faith." Furthermore, ethical deprogramming is not reverse proselytizing, a deliberate attempt to return a person to the original faith commitment before the cult commitment was entered into. Instead, it is an effort to give the cult member one more opportunity to return to his own personal choice, fully informed of what he is doing and why he might be choosing it.

Is deprogramming evil? Many parents would deny this, for they have seen their families reunited, both emotionally and physically, and often even spiritually, through a process that began with deprogramming. But the decision to deprogram is never arrived at easily or quickly by parents; the investment of emotions is usually much greater than the investment of money. The parents of Mary Beth were concerned about their daughter in late 1975; she had been working as a public relations representative for a major cult among the members of Congress and their staffs. When she refused to come home for Christmas because she "had too much important work to do," the parents applied some emotional pressure and worked a compromise: Mary Beth would return home for one week after New Year's Day. Her parents described the events surrounding Mary Beth's deprogramming and the results of that deprogramming:

> Mary Beth arrived on a Saturday night, . . . and we kept her busy so she would not contact the local [organization] centers. On Monday her mother went to the courthouse with her attorney and obtained a conservatorship order *ex parte*. Mary Beth was with me, and as soon as I knew the order had been signed by the judge, I took her to a motel. The conservatorship was served on her, and she became extremely agitated.
>
> Since she had been in the movement for six and a half years, we had contracted for the services of a well-known deprogrammer, and had him available at the motel at the time. After her first outburst, Mary Beth became totally silent, many times sitting under the desk in a fetal position, rocking back and forth and chanting. The first breakthrough didn't come until the fourth day, when Mary Beth first began to talk. We stayed in the motel for two more days, until Friday. On Friday afternoon Mary Beth and her mother left for the rehabilitation center. We did not realize at that time that she was partially faking, and she caused a great deal of concern on the plane trip. . . . Eventually they made it to the rehab center, and her counseling continued. On Monday morning, one week after her deprogramming had begun, she made the final break and became herself again. . . .
>
> Several things concerning Mary Beth's rescue deserve mention. It was a very difficult time for parents, both emotionally and physically. The commitment must be complete, or failure is almost assured. The deprogramming process was one of the most gentle, loving experiences I have ever experienced, and yet, since for most of the time we were talking to someone who was not my

stepdaughter, it was also extremely difficult. The emotional impact on parents and children is tremendous. And it doesn't end there. When the young cultist returns to reality, the depth of family love is also very heavy. Of course, that is on the positive side, but the impact is still very profound.

Also, Mary Beth, at the end of her deprogramming, became essentially the same person she was when she entered the group, and *reverted to behavior appropriate to a sixteen-year-old* [emphasis added]. The process of her growing into a twenty-four-year-old woman took appreciably longer than the deprogramming and rehabilitation, lasting for almost one year. It takes some time for the ex-cultist to reestablish the decision-making processes, and to catch up emotionally and psychologically with their chronological growth.

Mary Beth was very angry and vitriolic at the beginning, and we thought that there would never be a time when we could be friends again. Now, however, she is very grateful that we made the attempt and were successful, and our relationship is *very* close. She says that without our help she would have never been able to make the break away from the group, even though a part of her always felt that she did not want to be there.[19]

Whether a cultist leaves a group through some sort of voluntary escape, such as walking away, or through deprogramming, the need to begin some type of rehabilitation therapy is immediate. Rehabilitation, or "rehab," is best done in an atmosphere apart from home; it is designed to help the former cult member adjust to society, reestablish family relationships, share his experiences with peers also going through rehabilitation, and to accept himself while also accepting exactly what he did to himself. A strong effort must be made to assist the individual in relearning the decision-making process; so many decisions are made for cult members that major decisions such as vocational goals for life and even simple matters of deciding what clothes to wear at a particular time are equally difficult.[20] The former member is encouraged and guided in restructuring his life for the future by reassessing personal and career goals, while also offered the opportunity to nourish a sense of healthy theological inquiry. Residual sexual problems must be dealt with. While some groups create massive guilt feelings about anything sexual according to their strict standards, other groups reach the opposite extreme and encourage, or even require, promiscuity (i.e., "flirty fish"). In either case, the individual must be helped to reevaluate his sexual feelings in the light of his escape from the cult. People undergoing rehabilitation are *not* either physical or emotional invalids being treated in a hospital. They are people who need help and direction in reestablishing their lives, but those of us who know such individuals do not need to feel overly concerned about pampering them; in fact, pampering could sometimes prove to be the worst thing we could do for someone who is relearning some of the basics of life in our society.

Rehabilitation should be a family affair, and with good reason. Parents are often tormented by nagging questions such as "What did we do wrong?" Whether the answer lies in something they actually did or in the effective recruitment techniques of the cults, the family needs to discuss the anguish of the experience. It is helpful for them to discover each other's emotional ties with the cult member (and thereby their commitment to love him), and to be counseled in how to overcome their feelings of guilt and their pain. Mutual respect and shared humility are two virtues that should be eagerly sought by all involved in the family's anguish. The length of time required by an individual to reorder his life is a highly personal variable; but each day apart from the cult involvement represents one step forward toward a new life.

Rehabilitation is absolutely necessary to help thwart "quick recapture" or relapse into cult activity that arises from sources outside of the control of the former member. People who have recently left a cult are often called "floaters" because of the danger that they might rejoin, or float back into, the group because of the residual effects of the cult on that person's life. Rehabilitation helps to prevent this, in part because it fills time constructively, thereby removing some of the dangers implicit in idleness. Rehabilitation also helps to reinforce the deprogramming work by giving a backstop against a cult member's faking of an effective deprogramming, as we already have seen can happen. The problems that floaters must face are greater than those we saw earlier: meeting former members on the street, reading the same translation of the Bible, etc. Cults will often go to great lengths to try to recapture fallen members, usually through emotional or spiritual threats. Rehabilitation affords the ex-cultist an opportunity to learn about these guises, recognize them, and then to be able to make a careful response, which is free from fear or other manipulation. For example, veiled telephone threats to former members are not uncommon.[21] To be effective, rehabilitation cannot be a casual counseling relationship. Those entering into a rehabilitation situation must be willing to devote upwards of one year on a regular and frequent basis with the person who is seeking reentry into society.

One word of caution on rehabilitation is necessary. The cult member has just come through a traumatic experience of cult membership, which was based, at least in part, on some sort of religious convictions. While it is vital to work toward reestablishing a healthy relationship with God (and Christ for those of Christian persuasion), this aspect of rehabilitation usually cannot be rushed; a spirit of inquiry must be encouraged, as well as a desire to trust others in religious matters. It is *not* enough in the overwhelming majority of cases, nor would it be desirable, simply to read the Bible and seek to proselytize a person toward his former religion. This return to one's former religious beliefs, if it occurs at all, requires the one great factor that all men find helpful for healing: time.

Perhaps the best form of religious rehabilitation is patient praying and reading Scripture together while discussing the contents and perhaps its implications. Rehabilitation is meant to restore a person's ability to make a free choice, both intellectually and emotionally, about his relationship with God. Any attempt to be anything other than objective and informational may be met with a great deal of resistance. Don't forget that a former cult member joined the cult through an initial expression of curiosity and trust; he may feel hesitant about expressing those same feelings toward another person who is seeking to instill a religious awareness. While a natural curiosity about religion will probably reappear with effective rehabilitation, the level of trust required takes a considerable amount of time to establish.

Of course, there are exceptions to every rule, as we have seen many times before. Several former cult members credit the power of prayer for their escape, and this must never be overlooked or shortchanged. One member of an exotic eastern group went through deprogramming three times, with absolutely no apparent success. However, he was finally driven to such a serious condition by the people in his religion that he sought out a clergyman who possessed what only could be called a highly professional ministry of exorcism. This cult member went through a dramatic exorcistic rite and emerged with the same sort of freedom of mind that a person who has been successfully deprogrammed usually enjoys. While this ex-cultist still had to undergo extensive rehabilitation, his "rehab" was built around another profound religious experience, which freed him *from* what he had come to perceive as the bondage of the cult *for* a chance to seek the new life he wanted.[22]

It is also wise for professionals and parents to encourage

whatever intellectual curiosity the young adult might express about his experiences. Quite often, rehabilitated young people want to "go public" with their stories, and this can be an essential part of reinforcing rehabilitation therapy. This has another beneficial effect; it minimizes any efforts the cult might make to regain its former member or to cause him either physical or emotional harm. Of course, the most important and beneficial effect of "going public" should be most obvious; nothing tells of the dangers of the cults more effectively than a first-person account.

chapter 9

The Legal Battle

Almost everyone in America knows that our Constitution expressly protects freedom of religion, primarily as a result of the colonists' yearning for a land where they would not be constrained to practice a religion forced upon them by the government of the nation. But *religion is NOT the primary issue* in the legal battle. The focal point of the legal question is the freedom of the individual's mind. Even two hundred years ago, Thomas Jefferson put his finger precisely on the problem at hand today. "Almighty God hath created the mind free, *and manifested his supreme will that free it shall remain.*"[1]

The cults are seeking protection under the First Amendment for both their religious beliefs and their religious practices. Religious values and beliefs have always been afforded protection under the Constitution, but are religious practices given the same protection? Or should a balancing test be applied that would examine the threshold issue of the harmfulness of the techniques used both in obtaining and maintaining control over members?[2] Certainly the legal opinions of lawyers who profess knowledge of the basic issues are sharply divided. A prominent ACLU lawyer, who has represented several cult cases, as well as other cases that have involved freedom of expression, sees cult groups as an aid to

American culture. "The First Amendment doesn't care, as an abstract principle, whether they are regarded by anyone as good or bad. People are entitled to join these groups and come and go and believe what they will and worship as they please or not, regardless of anyone's opinion as to whether it's a good thing or bad for society in general."[3] However, the cult member murdered at the airport in Jonestown, Guyana was not free "to come and go" as she pleased.

Another American Civil Liberties Union attorney, a national officer of the organization, has a mixed personal reaction toward the new religions; he doesn't find their theologies appealing, but he sees nothing harmful in their operations.

> For myself, I find the new religious groups very peculiar and unattractive. I have been unable to discover, however, any techniques of persuasion employed by them that are more sinister than the Catholic Church employs in respect to novitiates. . . .[4]

As should be obvious to almost anyone, the analogy of the Roman Catholic novitiate does not stand up to consideration for several reasons, the most important of all being the continual process of screening that such novitiates undergo and cult members appear not to enjoy, as well as the periods of release from the responsibilities of the novitiate, set apart to allow the freedom to evaluate one's commitment before making it a life profession. In addition, the Roman Catholic Church does not go out on street corners to attract members of religious orders, nor do Catholics hide the religious nature of their organization when they do recruit.

But the second problem with this position, stated by a high ACLU official, reflects a serious defect in the entire approach to the legal question that many libertarians are assuming. Why is it that civil libertarians are so loath to appear to even consider the experiences of numerous people who allege that they were "taken in" by some of these religious groups through the use of front organizations, which deny that their group enjoys even a hint of religiosity?[5]

The outrage expressed by libertarians over the possible misuses of deprogramming has not been matched by anything more than a whisper of an effort, if even that, to either substantiate or investigate the allegations of antilibertarian activities perpetrated by the cults. The primary motivator for this double standard is viewed by many to be the ACLU.[6] This group has made a vigorous and one-sided study of the most volatile surface issue, deprogramming, but it has also sidestepped any serious attempt to answer the more difficult questions of the constitutional rights of individual members. Have these concerned libertarians made any attempt to suggest who, if not their own organizations, should make the effort to prove or to disprove the allegations?

Furthermore, with respect to the statement of the ACLU leader, it is unreasonable to compare the loss of independent thinking to the doctrines of other religions.[7] For example, the Supreme Pontiff of the Roman Catholic Church may speak with all the authority of his office on issues of faith and morals when he speaks *ex cathedra* ("from his seat"). But such statements are meant as guidelines and do not affect the overall independence of the mind; this independence could easily be documented by the apparently vast number of Roman Catholics who willingly use methods of birth control that are not approved by the church, in spite of the moral authority of the Pope and his unequivocal pronouncements on this matter. In fact, Pius XII, an earlier Pope, who died in 1958, made a firm statement about the need of the human mind to remain independent:

> And just as it is illicit to appropriate another's goods or to make an attempt on his bodily integrity without his consent, so it is not permissible to enter into his inner domain against his will, whatever is the technique or method used.[8]

Another individual possessing impressive credentials, who has been making blanket statements urging approval of the practices of religious cults, is the vice chairman of the Philadelphia, Pennsylvania, chapter of a group that calls itself the Alliance for the Preservation of Religious Liberties (APRL). While some critics of APRL allege that it is cult sponsored,[9] APRL's denials of this allegation do not closely fit their other actions. Professing to sponsor efforts at reuniting families, the primary goal of APRL seems to be the desire to defend the right of the cults to exist and to proceed about their business unhampered by their critics. Their vigorous protests have been seen at meetings of parents who desire to share information about the cults and to support each other; APRL has attempted to disrupt such free public gatherings in private hired halls.

The concerns of APRL for cult affairs can be seen in the names of people whom they list as directors of local chapters, including members of religious groups who allege persecution, and lawyers for several well-known new religious groups. Even more interesting are the noncult names listed at times on APRL's letterhead. In 1977, they listed a Roman Catholic bishop from Michigan, who never gave them permission to use his name and who asked them to delete it from their publicity, which they promptly did.[10] One member of their board is listed as a "Rev." with a denominational affiliation in the Episcopal Church; however, there is no record of any such person in the official journals of the Episcopal Church, which record the names of those properly ordained.[11]

But what about the viewpoint of the vice chairman of the Philadelphia chapter of APRL? This man, formerly a fundamentalist Baptist who apparently abandoned that line of theology and adopted the philosophies of a cult leader,[12] states that "a person's right to worship as he or she pleases is guaranteed by the First Amendment to the Constitution of the United States. It therefore follows that deprogramming of a human being, no matter who assists in the act, constitutes a criminal act. No court in this land has any evidence that brainwashing, kidnapping, or deprogramming goes on in the new religions."[13] Another observer of the religious scene, a Los Angeles psychologist, stated that "we are guaranteed by the Constitution of the United States to be able to practice religion whatever it might be, in the fashion we so choose."[14]

But does the Constitution actually mean to imply that we have both the freedom to *believe* and the freedom to *practice* our beliefs? In spite of the protestations of people either sympathetic to the cults or actually involved in such groups, the courts have generally held that the freedom to practice religious beliefs has always been conditioned by the basic question of whether the practice gives rise to any danger either to society or to the individual. The interest of the religious group must be weighed against the state's legitimate interest in regulating or forbidding the activity.

This principle can be demonstrated easily by examining groups that place their primary emphasis on belief in Satan as their main deity and who also hold that the practice of human sacrifice is essential to keep their god satisfied. Such groups actually do exist in this country, and their right to *believe* as they do is absolutely protected by the Constitution. But can we actually agree, as spokesmen for cult groups claim, that the right to conduct worship that involves human sacrifice is protected by the Constitution? Are we saying that murder is legal when it is done in the performance of religious practices? Are we saying that a person has the right to give his consent to his own murder at the hands of other people?

Many legal experts would argue that the state has the responsibility to prohibit such practices for the safeguarding both of the individual and of society. The state's concern would have to include several areas: whether or not the religious practices involved precipitated any psychiatric or physical disorders; whether teachings of a group led to such feelings of guilt that suicide or self-mutilation became a serious factor in the group's membership; whether members suffer from maturational arrest in language, thought, or experience; whether physical disease or injury is caused (including that inflicted through poor diet, lack of sleep, harmful practices such as sniffing of toluene, and the loss of menstral cycle); and whether members are deprived of adequate medical attention.[15]

The problems that would arise with the free practice of human sacrifice are analogous to the problems with the cults. Despite the denials of cult leaders and attorneys, many former cult members themselves, as well as psychiatrists who have treated cult members, state that the minds of cult members were under some means of control from outside their person, which inhibited them from practicing either freedom of thought or association, once they were enmeshed in the workings of the cult. The cults consistently counter this assertion with the claim that the person made a free choice to come to the first, second, or third sessions; this early commitment would therefore demonstrate that the recruit expressed the initial freedom of association. However, once a person is assimilated into the cult, voluntary withdrawal is next to impossible for all but the strongest, those who have been able to maintain some sense of personal, emotional, and intellectual integrity. The fact that some cults recruit deceptively or apply subtle techniques to bring about what might be considered unholy conversions has already been demonstrated above; the presence of these techniques suggests that the indoctrination processes carried out by the cults are not fully consensual.[16] Simply stated, the inductee is not aware at all times of what he is getting into; the end results that the group seeks to accomplish are not fully revealed, as they would be in a group such as the Roman

Catholic Church. If the inductee is not aware, either through deception or subtle techniques, which build up in stages, how could he be said to have given his fully informed consent?

Parents have continually asked cult leaders to allow them access to their children, who are almost always of legal age, for a period of time to give an opportunity for conversation and understanding to emerge. If the children are indeed *not* victims of mind control but are in a totally voluntary association with the religious group, why are the cults so adverse to offering a "cooling off" period where the convert can go home and prove to his parents that he is not at all a victim of coercion but actually acting out of his own free will? However, often under the guise of "important work for God," the cults frequently deny parents the privilege of extended visits with their children, unless the parents themselves are also members of the cult or are sympathetic. Although children may sometimes be offered the guise of freedom to visit their parents, they are usually unlikely to do so because they have come to believe that trafficking with their parents is akin to flirting with the devil. This allows the cults to enjoy the surface appearance of innocence because they can attribute the failure of children to maintain contact with their parents to the children's personal choice. The irony, of course, is that the children's choice has already been predetermined by the cult.

The constitutional rights of cult members may be violated in another way that is even more subtle than freedom of thought, religion, or association. The United States Constitution, as well as state constitutions and many state laws, forbids involuntary servitude. Once a person's mind and will is subdued to the point of being responsive only to the leaders of a religious organization, as cult critics contend, the member is then placed in a position where almost everything that he does for the group could conceivably be considered as involuntary servitude.[17] Cults keep their members busy, often with eighteen or more hours a day devoted directly to group concerns. In one group, approximately 70 percent of each waking day is estimated to be spent in fund raising among members who are relatively new and not advanced in the group, with most of the remaining time spent in continued mind suppression, "witnessing," and miscellaneous work and chores performed directly for the benefit of the group.[18] If there were not a capturing of the mind and will by these organizations, the circumstances of the young victims would be entirely different; however, the question must be asked whether acts performed under such allegedly extreme mental manipulation, entered into without fully informed prior consent, could be considered voluntary.

Another key legal issue for both parents and the cults is whether the seizure of a cult member constitutes kidnapping ("to seize and hold by force or fraud, as for ransom") or rescue ("to free or save from danger"). In a December 1974 California case, the court ruled that "parents may legally justify kidnapping an adult child 'if the parents have a reasonable belief' that their child is not able to make a free, voluntary, knowledgeable decision to stay within the so-called community." While this decision was appealed and upheld, it must *not* be taken as permission for parents to kidnap a consenting adult. However, a New York State court has delivered a similar opinion. A cult member was kidnapped from his group's training center in Westchester County, New York, for an attempt at deprogramming. The Westchester County grand jury refusal to indict the alleged kidnappers was based on justification. The district attorney explained that "Implicit in their [the grand jury's] findings was the belief that the family had the right to take reasonable steps to rescue the child from a situation which they believed constituted a danger to his health and welfare."[19]

"Conservatorship" is another key concept in the legal clouds surrounding cult members, their parents, and the "kidnapping" issue. Should the parents of a child who is no longer a minor have the right to petition the courts to order the removal of their adult child from a cult until it can be determined whether the child is indeed using his own free will? Should that same parent have the legal right to petition to be placed in a guardianship role over the child's assets, to protect the child's financial position from the financial pressures of the group? It is around this particular issue that some courts have been giving directives that indicate that young adults can indeed be seized against their wills. "Where the individual has been rendered mentally disordered as a result of his brainwashing experience," attorney Richard Delgado suggests a simple solution: declare the child incompetent.[20] However, Delgado also notes the fact that mind manipulation is so powerful that it is possible to produce a person with a mind that is totally manipulated but whose exterior appearances, gestures, and utterances, seem totally normal. In other words, it is possible for a person to be programmed to appear "normal." Delgado maintains that a seemingly stable, enduring person can be produced by cult indoctrination who will resist returning to his former life and who also will refuse to consider the changes perpetrated on his person as harmful.

Some individuals have used force, in accordance with court-ordered directives, to enforce conservatorship decisions. There have been several instances where the only means of enforcing a conservatorship has been through a "rescue," which the cults call a "kidnapping"; however, such tactics have occasionally proven to be the only means of facilitating a determination as to whether or not a young person is indeed exercising total freedom of thought and association, as his cult asserts, or whether he is under duress and mind control, as the parents claim.

In attempting to sort through which new religions and religious leaders are authentic and which exist primarily to "fill their coffers with money,"[21] the courts may have to determine when conservatorships are desirable, as well as when deprogramming might be a justifiable action to take. In a United States district court decision, the judge described justification of kidnapping an adult child as "the defense of necessity," where "the parents who would do less than what the parents did for their daughter . . . would be less than responsible, loving parents."[22]

In another decision handed down in a United States district court, the judge ruled that a mother's hiring of deprogrammers to rescue her child from a cult arose "not from her abhorrence of the religious group *per se,* but rather directly from the solicitude that a mother holds for her daughter's health and well-being. Defendents (the deprogrammers), as agents of the mother, derived their motivation from this same maternal solicitude."[23]

There are two other factors in the legal entanglements related to cults that should draw considerable attention. A few cults have quite elaborate corporate structures, which are often designed to direct funds toward political causes or the direct personal gain of the leaders. If these allegations are true, as some observers and defectors allege, should these groups be allowed to maintain their status as either religious or nonprofit corporations, and therefore be allowed to continue a preferred tax status on incomes that are not directly related to religious purposes? The manner in which these groups try to bend the tax laws to their advantage is remarkable. One cult has made the claim to the Internal Revenue Service that it is a church; but this same group makes a claim to the contrary in its recruiting literature—that it is not a church at all but rather a "Bible research and study fellowship." Another organization lost the exempt status of several major property holdings in New York City and the surrounding area because the property in question was not used primarily for religious purposes but rather for the commercial and political interests of the group, including one of New York City's three daily morning newspapers.

Several cults have been confronted with lawsuits for the alleged deception and/or emotional torture of members. In one case, a quadriplegic gave over two hundred and ten thousand dollars to a cult on the alleged promise that he would be healed within one year; the amount given represented the cost of two automobiles given to cult leaders and a percentage of the total monetary award he received as a result of the accident. The cult confirmed that they received the funds but claimed it was a donation given to the cause. After the religious group filed an eight hundred thousand dollar countersuit, the case was settled out of court.

The legal questions surrounding the cults will keep a host of lawyers busy for many years. One cult member wins a suit against her parents for attempting to deprogram her. A group is barred from soliciting through the mails because the funds collected were not used for the purposes advertised; that same group's seminary was refused accreditation by the New York State Board of Regents, and this educational decision will probably be appealed in the courts. A cult spokesman has filed a $30 million lawsuit against a United States congressman and the House of Representatives subcommittee he chairs for allegedly depriving the group's spokesman of his constitutional rights of freedom of speech and freedom of religion.[24] The initiators of such suits have occasionally described their legal actions as creative and legitimate means for fund raising. Other groups deny their members the privilege of possessing a driver's license, forcing them to drive illegally; their only reason for this is that an age must be declared on an application, and their members have assumed new names and are, therefore, eternal. "Flirty fish" are encouraged into prostitution, an illegal activity, while other members of the same group go about stealing to support their communes or cells. The legal problems raised are endless.

So the debate will rage. Civil libertarians counter the concerns of cult parents and sympathetic judges with lofty statements that could apply equally both to people concerned about proper deprogramming and to those who are alleged to manipulate persons into a conversion that is not totally free of coercive persuasion. But the questions raised by libertarians almost always are directed solely toward the deprogrammers rather than the religious groups. Are we free to do whatever we want, in the guise of religion?

A basic question is who has the right to decide matters of conscience for someone else. Can someone attempt to force young people of legal age into a pattern of religious belief, without denying the constitutional guarantee of freedom of religion? According to one libertarian, this type of unchecked action can only lead to an American society in which religious liberty is nothing more than a memory.[25] But *what* is to remain unchecked? Should it be the practices of legitimate deprogrammers, acting on the behalf of parents who seek to ensure that their children are allowed freedom of thought and association? Or should the coercive persuasion of some groups, often employed openly, be allowed to continue unchecked?

Spokesmen on all sides of the issue agree that the freedom of the mind is the cornerstone of the overall question. Speaking at a conference sponsored by the American Civil Liberties Union, a spokesman for the National Council of Churches stated that "One can criticize and reject the content of one of these or any faith group while still defending their right to exist, to preach their views, to seek converts, and to try to retain their adherents as long as they do not use force, coercion, or duress."[26]

Whether force, coercion, or duress is used is a central question; the cult leaders deny allegations made by former members and even by reporters who have infiltrated the groups. Benjamin Cardoza, a former Supreme Court justice, recognized as early as 1928 that man is free only if he knows, and "so in proportion to our knowledge." Cardoza saw no freedom without choice, and no choice without knowledge. His conclusion is that the mind is in chains whenever it is without the opportunity to choose.[27]

But the ultimate example of the paradox that religious freedom in the cults presents to the legal community has been saved for last; it appears to rest in the mind of a nationally recognized lawyer for a particular cult, who is also on the board of directors for the Alliance to Preserve Religious Liberty.

In a statement issued in the ACLU documentation on deprogramming, he wrote of how the "searchlight of truth [must] be focused on the activities of those individuals who are forcefully attempting to change the ideas of this country's most valuable assets [our youth]."[28] However, this same distinguished attorney was also a guest on a nationally syndicated television interview show, which was aired about the same time that the ACLU conference on deprogramming was held, in early 1977. When asked whether the issues involved in deprogramming and the accusations of brainwashing were complex enough that the courts should set some firm guidelines relative to the freedoms of thought and association and alleged brainwashing, his answer was a definite "yes." He paused for a moment, and then added the following conclusion: ". . . except in areas which relate to religious beliefs."[29]

chapter 10

Helping the Kids

There are several relatively direct precautions that parents, churches and synagogues, and the young people themselves can take to help keep a person's mind his own and to avoid falling into a religious experience that might not be to his best interests. Young people themselves should be encouraged to follow these five steps, for their own soul's benefit:

BE PREPARED

A person should know what he believes about God, and why he believes it. Children should be encouraged to discuss doubts and other questions with parents, clergy, and other professionals; these people, in turn, must not push aside such inquiries as merely childish wonderings. If you believe in God, why do you believe? If you say that the Bible is an important source of direction for your life, do you know what it is in the Bible that applies to you? Could someone come along and start to quote passages out of context, and perhaps destroy what little understanding you had?

No one, whatever his religious background, is safe from a cult. While some studies suggest that Jewish and Roman Catholic backgrounds are most frequently represented among the backgrounds of the members of certain groups, even Christians from traditions that are totally biblical in their orientation have been proven to be vulnerable. Going through the sacramental rites of our religious heritage is insufficient protection from life's trials and challenges, much less from the assault of an articulate cult recruiter. Young people must persist in the study of the Scriptures of their faith, never ceasing to make inquiry.

BE WARY

When someone approaches you with the solutions to the problems of the world, invites you to lectures or retreats, is generally either unemployed or not a student, but yet appears to have spiritual insights, beware! Such people may have no connections with any cult; they may be totally innocent of any wrongdoing and genuinely motivated. But investigate their claims and their associations before accepting any offers. Likewise, beware of discussion or study groups that claim to be nonsectarian. While such groups do exist, many "nonsectarian" or "nondenominational" groups actually prove to be the most narrow-minded and sectarian of all! Remember that some groups offer attractive-sounding intellectual pursuits as their initial entry for recruiting on college campuses; also remember that these recruiters will often tell flagrant falsehoods to avoid revealing the religious nature of the organization that is sponsoring such intellectual pursuits.

AVOID

Be cautious around people who approach you and are not affiliated in a concrete way with your academic community, military organization, or place of business; these people may be recruiters for cults. Find out whether they have a *bona fide* association with your school, such as a current student identification card, or whether they are fellow members of the armed forces. Beware also of people who have no apparent source of income, whether parental support or gainful employment; they may receive their support from a religious group. Avoid people who encourage the study of a particular guru or teacher, and most especially those who evidence antagonism toward the religious views of more traditional religious groups or parents.

RESEARCH AND MOVE SLOWLY

If you attach yourself to a group and are suspicious of the atmosphere the group is creating, avoid making any sort of commitment that cannot be escaped easily. Avoid "salesmanship" pressures that might lead to a statement of commitment, as well as any profession of commitment that is made under any type of emotional pressure or under circumstances that might suggest to you that the leaders are attempting to inflict undue outside influence on you.

Never cease to use your intellectual capacities for independent inquiry; never accept something as legitimate scholarship or "biblical research" simply because someone assures you that it is! If a group discourages you from asking questions or postpones giving answers ("Someone tomorrow will be better able to answer your question"), then you probably have encountered a cult. Ask others. Do your own research. Is the group known to the campus chaplains or the local clergy? Evaluate the information offered you and make your own judgment, relying on your intellectual resources as well as on your emotional resources and needs.

WATCH FOR REVELATION AND MIRACLES

"Signs and wonders" are still very common today in a number of legitimate expressions of religious activity, particularly Christianity. However, even something, which on the surface may appear to be a great spiritual blessing, can eventually prove to be a counterfeit; there exist in most religions some people who are not properly motivated, wolves in sheep's clothing. Be wary of groups that promise answers to prayer or to share divine revelations either for payments made to the group or for the surrender of property. When "signs and wonders," such as miracles of healing, are reported, evaluate them under strict standards of discernment. Are the events related accurately? Is there some medical evidence to attest to conditions both before and after the miracle? Check also the terminology of the group; when the cult uses theological terms, do they mean the same thing that you do?

But what if . . .

Even the person who responds with extreme caution to the approaches of someone offering a new religious experience may find himself drawn inadvertently into a cult. Avoiding the pressures of joining a cult requires the same sort of concentration and care needed to avoid catching the flu in the middle of winter. Precautions must be taken, but most of them amount to little more than "common sense." And, just as a person can sense that he might be catching the flu by the power of observation, a person can also be trained to observe and to check himself for symptoms of cult involvement. In the same manner, parents and other professionals can observe young people and watch for the following symptoms; all too often, they are a certain indication that a person has come into some degree of association with a cult.

A SUDDEN CHANGE IN BEHAVIOR PATTERNS

Have you suddenly found yourself abandoning your former interests or adding a wealth of new and seemingly exciting activities? Have you lost your desire to remain at home (or in a dormitory) most evenings in favor of going to a regular series of meetings with your new friends? Can you sense something different about your personality? Have you lost your sense of humor or even your sense of integrity? Are you finding yourself doing things, whether "good" or "bad," which are somehow just not the "normal" you?

A BREAKDOWN IN COMMUNICATION

How well are you communicating with your parents and friends, your spouse, or even your roommates? Have you become secretive or defensive about things happening in your life? Numerous parents have reported that their children, during the process of integration into a cult, tend to become very secretive and even more defensive about new friends and interests. This is a symptom of the initial stages of recruitment, when the cult leaders deliberately attempt to isolate and alienate the potential member to ensure the cult's attractiveness to, and control over, the subject.

A SUDDEN RUSH OF NEW FRIENDS

Many major cults, whether they recruit openly or under the cover of a nonreligious-front organization, train their members carefully in methods of winning friends and, in turn, new members. Whether this might be called "evangelism," "witnessing and undershepherding," "love bombing," or any other term, it should be evaluated carefully as to its motivations and sources.

Do your new friends call you two or three times a day to see how you are doing? Do they show an excessive amount of concern for you? While such concern might seem like "love" and "caring," make certain that it is genuine love and caring and not just a concerted effort to gain and maintain your attention and also your approval of the group.

If you are naturally gregarious, you may find that meeting new friends is an easy and enjoyable task. But if you tend to be more withdrawn or slower to make deep, trusting relationships, be careful when you find yourself drawn into a group because of peer pressure expressed in such simple phrases as "Gee, you are a wonderful person," or "That's a great idea you just had," or "We sure know how you feel, and we agree with you completely." While such expressions may be honest reflections of real feelings, there have been many reported instances of people who might normally resist being drawn into a group of new people who have been enticed to enlist through such direct statements of appreciation or encouragement. Once again, such statements may not be evil; observe how they fit into the other attributes of the group's behavior and reaction to you.

THINKING SOCIETY IS EVIL

Have things that once seemed good to you now taken on the appearance of evil? Of course, such revelations may be authentically from God. But exactly what is your new group of friends describing as evil? Have they split the world into two camps, "us" and "them," with only people who think a certain way ("us") described as "good"? Are you being led to think that your parents or other family members are evil because they are not in the group? Have you found your moral behavior suddenly shifting, more out of fear of the devil than from a healthy source of discipline or behavior that is changed by God? Do your new friends ever suggest that all society is evil, that all government is corrupt unless it is controlled by people who believe as the group believes, or that all churches must be evil because they don't agree with your new group? All of these are symptoms of encroaching cult involvement.

INVITATION TO A WEEKEND THAT NEVER ENDS

Are your new friends inviting you to a weekend retreat? Are you providing your own transportation, so you can leave if and when you wish? Are you paying your own way, or is the group sponsoring you for some reason? If you have already gone on such a weekend adventure, are you willing to share what you experienced with others outside the group, including your parents, or are you secretive or defensive about your experiences? Have you enjoyed a comfortable weekend, with enough sleep, a good diet that not only tastes good and is filling but is also well balanced, a sense of personal dignity and privacy, the ability to express questions and negative thoughts?

In a similar vein, you should beware of changes in spending habits. Are you suddenly being encouraged to give a percentage of your income to the group? Have you become so interested in your new friends and their thinking that you are saving money or gathering funds in any way possible so that you may take one of their courses to get the basic message? Some groups charge a hundred dollars or more for their initial courses, and members are under constant pressure to subscribe to more advanced courses in order to learn "greater truth." Don't forget that the Gospel of Jesus Christ is a *free* gift of God's grace and love to you! You do not need to pay for it in order to receive it![1]

THE LACK OF RATIONAL IDEAS

What happens when others ask you questions about your involvement in a new religious experience or some esoteric group? Are you able to present concepts and ideas to others about your experience that are rational? Or can you only parrot Scriptures that the group has taught you? Even if you are good at quoting Scriptures, are you adept at using any translation of the Bible to illustrate or to prove your viewpoint? Or is your ability confined to the Scripture used exclusively by the cult, in which you have been rehearsed? Can you take a cult dogma and offer a rational explanation for it, or is it "just that way" because that is how you have been taught it, and for no other reason?

If you feel that you are showing some of these symptoms, or if someone whom you know has these symptoms, you should seek outside guidance to insure that whatever group you have encountered is legitimate in its concern for you, that it has a religious orientation that produces good fruit both in its members and in society at large, that it functions without any guise of deception, and that you can leave the group at any time, without fear or threat, physical harm, inconvenience, or emotional damage. If you cannot be certain about these factors, the safest course may be to avoid contact with the group until you are absolutely certain about its legitimacy.

chapter 11

What Can Be Done?

Postscript to Churches (and Synagogues)

What can the gathering of God's people, which calls itself the Church, in its hundreds of manifestations as local churches and denominations, do to respond to the problem of cult religions? For that matter, what can members of the various expressions of Judaism do within their religious structures to help confront the problems presented by deceptive religions-for-profit?

The Church is a giant, albeit a drowsy one! We have millions of members who have been called by God and empowered by his Holy Spirit to do a mighty work in this world; we are to stand fast, in a holy manner, against anything that is not of God. It would be easy to point the finger of self-accusation at the Church, or at any particular denomination, pointing out numerous instances where the Church has failed in its mission. But this self-flagellation is not the most constructive answer available. It is true that the Church does not always teach the rudiments of faith to its members, be they young or old. We are often lax in our prayer, both with our members and for our members. Youth ministry that reaches the age-groups most vulnerable to cult membership efforts is too often a low priority in our commitments of both time and money. Stated in another manner, we do not always

156

love our children as much as we should, or as much as they need to be loved. What then can the Church, and to some degree also our Jewish brothers and sisters, do to help combat the nuisance of the cults, their powers over people, and the clear and present dangers with which they confront society? Here are some possible answers to a complicated question:

WE CAN DEVELOP A DEEPER LIFE IN OUR FAMILIES

Does the Church do all that it can to encourage family life together as a Christian family? Do we educate parents and children to understand all that this implies? Do we encourage parents and children to spend time together? Or do we, perhaps inadvertently, even schedule religious and business meetings in a way that supports the breakdown of the family unit? It would not be impossible for many churches to schedule most or even all meetings and week-night activities on the same evening, so that parents could come to activities together with their children and share "church night." Some religious groups stress that all members should hold free a particular evening of the week for "family night" at home, where the commitment of each family member is toward the nuclear family group and its common activities and needs.

Parents need to be able to appreciate their children as individuals with unique gifts and problems. Don't just love children by giving them material gifts! Parents can love children even more by giving them their time and attention, which is their life! This style of approach helps to maintain communication, while providing a framework for honest and open, loving yet free, relationships between parents and children.

Churches can encourage parents to do some of the simple, and almost obvious, things that will help keep a child free from a cult. Insist that the family eat at least one meal of the

day together around a common table; encourage the participation of each family member in the conversation. We can
teach parents how to develop a regular discipline of prayer
and Scripture study for the family.

One observer of American family life suggested that
churches should encourage parents to make the *house* much
more of a *home* for children, and that the fastest way to begin
to accomplish this quickly in some families would be to remove the plastic coverings from the furniture in the living
room. It is a sad commentary on American family life that
there is much truth in that remark. The Church must continually remind people that a house is not a home; furthermore, a Christian house is not necessarily a Christian home!
A group of professing Christians may be related together as a
nuclear family, live together under one roof, and possess all
the credentials for being Christian, but they do not automatically create a Christian *home* until their life together is un-
dergirded by mutual respect, a common prayer life, and the
feeling that everyone present is welcomed as a member of
the family and that the home is theirs.

THE CHURCH CAN SEEK OUT AND DEVELOP
EFFECTIVE ADULT LEADERSHIP

We have fallen into a deceptive trap whenever we equate effective leadership with professional leadership. When we
seek out leaders for any ministry, and most especially ministry to young people, we must first of all locate those people
who have the gift of leadership, which is anointed of God by
the Holy Spirit.

How many churches automatically expect the pastor to do
the youth work? But there is no guarantee that a seminary or
Bible-college education is a certain indication that a person
has been equipped by God for youth work! In fact, nothing
could be less true. Anyone, whether clergy or laity, can take a
class or attend a seminar to acquire the skills needed to com-

municate with young people, but the effectiveness of those skills will be *fully* manifested only through the persons whom God chooses to supervise and to direct youth ministry.

Young people need to be loved, and they can usually sense when a youth leader is disinterested in them. Our young people require and deserve much more than mere exposure to an artful display of professional skills; they need to be exposed, foremost of all, to God's love, shown to them through people who are willing both to *work with* young people and to *serve* them as God directs.

WE CAN DEVELOP A SENSE OF COMMUNITY

Young adults want to belong to something greater than themselves, some sort of group with which they can identify. But we fail the young people, and often ourselves, by herding them into groups segregated by age, as though people under age twenty-one have to be isolated from the other activities of the Church. One obvious result of this style of axiomatic age segregation is that the whole Body of believers suffers. Older people have a variety of gifts, whether spiritual or practical, that they can offer to young people; the reverse is also true. Young people may have a sense of energy, optimism, and faith that older people tend to feel has passed them by; the enthusiasm that young people can generate is often both contagious and healthy for the Church. Whenever various parts of the Church start acting like an eye of the Body and say to the hand, "I have no need of you," then the Church has started on its road to decay, because it is saying that it does not want to be the fully functioning Body of Christ on earth.[1]

But this is not to say that segregation by age is always a detriment to effective ministry. Young adults have questions to be answered that people of other ages might not be confronted by; they also have certain needs that are strikingly different from other age groups. The Church must also offer young people the opportunity to gather among their peers; these opportunities must be so attractive and meaningful that they will demand the attention of the young people more than almost every other activity. These gatherings will include naturally many means for expressing fellowship and social interaction, but the major portion of time involved should be spent in developing the spiritual health and well-being of these believers.

One prominent Jewish spokesman says that we must learn to "retail, rather than wholesale" religion to young adults as well as to other age groups. His plea for more one-on-one training and the expression of growing faith is exactly the sort of concept that finds itself in relatively small groups, where young people can both seek God and "be found of him." We can never deny that some of the secrets of God's love and active concern will be discovered in recreation and social activities, but a forum for the deeper matters of God must be provided on a regular basis. Many cults are able to offer a counterfeit religion and to escape detection because their recruits were never trained to recognize "the real thing." Bank tellers are taught how to recognize counterfeit money; should we send our children into the world any less armed for the spiritual encounters they will experience?

WE CAN DEVELOP A MINISTRY
TO CULT VICTIMS

Whenever one person joins a cult, the probability exists that a domino effect will be created, generating emotional, spiritual, and even physical turmoil not only on the cult inductee but also on his family and immediate friends. Parents are hit by a two-fold trauma: the grief of seeing a child disappear perhaps into the underground of a religious group, and the accompanying shock of how little can be done to help the situation. This trauma is not unlike the grief process that a family goes through when a loved one dies. First, there is shock

("How could this happen?"), followed by confusion ("What is this group all about? What should I do next?"). Guilt and anger soon appear ("I hate the people in that group! What did I ever do wrong as a parent?"), and finally helplessness ("I haven't heard from my child in two years, and I am at my wits' end. I don't know what to do.")[2]

These parents, friends, and even spouses need the pastoral ministry of the Church. Any pastoral ministry offered must be considered totally insensitive if the pastor is so ignorant that he can only reply with some empty statement, such as "Gee, that's too bad," or "It must be God's will." Would we offer such a callous reply to a person who has just discovered that a loved one died? Of course not! The need for an informed, compassionate ministry to cult victims is also an urgent and real priority for hundreds of families around the country who are at various levels of the grief process.

These people are just as much victims of the cults as the members themselves; they must not be classified automatically as paranoid, guilt-ridden parents who are suspicious of anything different, or who are only "emotionally helpless worriers," as some critics have portrayed them. We need to offer these special victims patience, understanding, and an abundance of informed counsel.

We must also consider our obligation to minister to people who themselves are coming out of a cult experience as members; their specific problems are just as urgent as our ministries in other areas, and their problems are often even more complex.

It is not enough to have an ecclesiastical leader appoint a clergyman as "advisor" on cult problems; this has happened in several parts of the country, with the result that pastoral disasters have emerged, perpetrated by clergy or other professionals who entered their advisorship ignorantly and remained ignorant of the issues at hand.

Money could be made available for the specialized training

that would enable some clergy to be effective in counseling cult dropouts or escapees. We need people with a strong pastoral commitment, who are articulate not only in psychology but also in theology and sociology, people who can help others sort through a plethora of complex feelings about what has happened, while at the same time helping them to redirect their lives and perhaps even helping them to find eventually a healthy relationship with God. The Church should make available its resources to help people find Christ with the freedom of inquiry and association that God intends all his creatures to enjoy.

WE MUST CONTINUALLY RETHINK OUR EDUCATIONAL EFFORTS

What exactly are we teaching our members, whether old or young? Are we concerned with instilling in our members guidelines for firm moral principles? Do we teach them the history of our traditions and the significance behind our symbols and ritual? Do we teach them not only to believe in God but also encourage them to have faith in God? In other words, are we educating our people in the total richness of what it means to be a Christian, or are we shirking some areas because they make us uncomfortable?

One facet of education that must constantly be examined is whether we are feeding our people *information* about God, or that same information accompanied by clear statements of the *implications* of what that proffered information should have on the practical aspects of life? Do we spend so much time talking *about* Jesus that the young people never truly *meet* the Messiah as Savior? Are we bashful about calling our people to a state of repentence for their sins, or have we perhaps gone so far as to eliminate sin as a problem for Christians?

Have we spent so much time teaching the history that surrounds biblical narratives that we have failed to make alive to our people the faith experiences of such great men of God as

Abraham, Moses, the Prophets, and the Apostles? Have we encouraged our people to have spiritual heroes whom they can emulate? Conversely, do we sometimes spend so much time emphasizing the emotional aspects of faith that we tend to forget to encourage the development of spiritual and intellectual discipline?

The Church must take a strong stand on its own religion; we must teach people the fullness of the Faith, including its practical applications. The most urgent need of many Christians is how to be in touch with God through prayer, whether voicing our intercessions, giving thanks, confessing our sins, or discerning his will for our lives and the answers to our questions. We already have an abundance of theories about prayer and wonderful collections of prayer to which we can refer. But we must also know how to pray in the most practical, personal kind of way.

WE SHOULD ENCOURAGE VIABLE EXPERIENCES FOR CHRISTIAN SERVICE

Many cults promise opportunities for people to reach out and help others; sadly, those opportunities often prove to be only shadows of themselves, which serve primarily as recruiting attractions. However, this does not mean that we should shirk our responsibility to be the servants of God in a world that hungers not only for earthly bread but also for spiritual bread. Can the Church gather together some of its resources to create a helping ministry, a spiritual VISTA or Peace Corps, which idealistic people who are called to serve can work within? Or must we stick to the traditional models of the nineteenth century: church schools, choirs, guilds, and ushers only? There is nothing wrong with these functions and, in fact, there are many things right and essential about them. However, these traditional functions and ministries do not fit the emotional and spiritual needs of many young people, who desire to serve God and man together. Can't we expand our concern for missions, whether domestic or foreign, local or worldwide?

Nor can we look at a person who desires to serve God in his or her life and say, "Well, you should enter seminary and become ordained," or "Why don't you 'try your vocation' in a religious community?" What would happen to the ministry of the laity if everyone called to an active ministry for God entered seminary? Not only would lay ministry disappear or be emaciated, but the other results would be ruinous to the Church. In fact, the trend has already been established toward that ruination; based on current seminary enrollments and membership trends, within twenty years the Episcopal Church will have one ordained minister for each lay person. Other denominations are not far behind in this dubious pattern for ministry.

Perhaps the Church could take a stronger role in urging a revitalization of some of the governmental efforts to provide human service that have proven effective at some point in history, such as the Peace Corps or Volunteers in Service to America (VISTA). In spite of the administrative tangles and unhealthy dependency relationships that some such programs engender, perhaps even a marginal success rate might well be worth the effort.

WE CAN GATHER TO SHARE INFORMATION

The need for accurate information on new religions is great among individuals, private groups, and also within the various levels of government, whether agencies or legislatures. Too many people are making claims and assertions based solely on hearsay or opinion. A solidly documented, objective body of evidence should be accumulated before final judgments are made. It is a serious matter to accuse someone of deceptive recruiting techniques or financial chicanery; we must have some documentation to give strong substantiation to our evidence. We must not be allowed to convict people on our suspicions or feelings alone.

For example, several groups in this book have been accused of using deceptive techniques of recruiting and of using various methods of manipulating recruits into a state of coerced conversion. In all instances, examples have been offered, either from reports in the secular press or the religious media, or from primary resource materials including documents from the groups themselves and from the sworn statements of people who have been associated with the groups in question. I have heard literally hundreds of other instances of cult abuses, some poorly documented and some with no documentation at all; I have chosen only examples that are reliably documented and that reflect overall traits of the cult phenomenon. My strong suspicions about these other, undocumented, instances may be correct; but my suspicions are not sufficient as evidence to prove the alleged abuses. The Church should set these same standards.

WE COULD PRESS FOR VARIOUS REMEDIES THAT WOULD ALLOW THESE GROUPS TO CONTINUE

The Church has a strongly vested interest in the separation of church and state, including the various constitutional protections afforded religion. However, we also have a vested interest in preserving the entire integrity of the Constitution and our society, which allows us to believe as free individuals. We are allowed to be free in our thoughts and in our associations, or so the Founding Fathers who drafted the Constitution and the Bill of Rights desired.

Could it be that the question to be asked is not whether these cults should be allowed to continue, but rather whether the government has a right or an obligation to insure that steps are taken to resolve the complaints directed toward the cults?

One means of alleviating deceptive recruiting or fund raising might be to require members of any religious organization soliciting either contributions or individuals to identify both themselves and their parent organization in an open, complete, and honest manner at the onset of each recruiting or fund-raising contact. One particular group has hit upon the letter of this suggested law by requiring some of its members to wear name tags when soliciting in shopping-center parking lots; however this practice misses the spirit of disclosure that is needed. The name tags do bear the name of the organization, but the identifying factor in the organization's name is in extremely small print, while "Church" appears boldly across the bottom line.

Recruiters could be required to outline, at the beginning of their contact with a prospect, both the expectations that the group has of converts and the benefits that would be derived from membership. Too many people recruited into cults sense the excitement of the opportunities to serve God or other people and miss the implication that they may well be turned into fund raisers and recruiters themselves.

Most traditional religious communities offer, or even require, a "cooling off" period before final commitments can be made. Individuals are required to live away from the community and its members for a period of time that is long enough to allow careful consideration of the choice and commitment to be made. If coercion, indeed, was a factor in recruiting, this "isolation period" could help some people sort through the events surrounding their conversion.

Cults that require members to turn over all their wealth and earthly possessions could follow the lead of some religious communities and offer members the option of turning all or part of their earthly effects over to family or friends, rather than to the religious group. This would alleviate the fear of many that cults are more concerned for bodies and wealth accumulated for the benefit of the leadership than they are for the curing of souls. In a similar vein, any earthly riches, such as inheritance or other gifts, that the cult member receives could either be turned over to the group, kept in the possession of the individual member, or signed over to a family member or friend outside of the cult.

Public awareness of the questions that the cults pose must be strongly increased. Some school boards have expressed a strong concern about cults because members of their own families or people from their communities have been drawn off by groups; these school boards have had the courage to allow experts on certain aspects of the cult phenomenon to talk to classes or assemblies, even though, strictly speaking, such actions might be considered a violation of the separation of church and state. Churches can provide people with the expertise needed for this type of presentation, as well as for appearances on radio and television talk shows, which should include equal opportunity for expression of the cults' viewpoint. Churches must also take the lead in exposing their own members to the possible dangers of cults, recognizing this as a pastoral prophylaxis, which is required because almost anyone could be vulnerable to recruitment at certain moments in life.

WHAT WILL WE STAND FOR?

Young people, and many of their parents, desire a greater religious experience than sermons and classes, which appear to draw their primary inspiration from the op-ed pages of the nearby metropolitan newspaper. Conservative churches are growing, in part because they take a point of reference (the Bible) and make their unwavering stand on it. Cults grow for a similar reason; they take their point of reference, whether a unique scripture of their own or the leader's interpretation of the Bible, and stand on it, however strange or illogical it may appear to be.

Is there a greater absolute we can stand on than the current political or sociological, or even psychological theory? If we continue to build our houses of faith on sand, which shifts with every gust of wind; deriving our teachings from the fresh bursts of "creative" theological thinking, which may be proven either outmoded or totally in error within the next ten years; then how will we ever offer our people a stable faith to live by? Jesus Christ is the same, yesterday, today, and forever. That might be either boring or inconsequential for those people who would prefer to mold God to their own image, and that is their privilege. But it is a firm foundation for many to build a lasting relationship with God that will allow people to grow fully into the image of God in which they were created. This foundation will not collapse under the stress of alleged scholarship; people have tried hard to disprove the Resurrection, but none have succeeded.

FIVE POPULAR NEW RELIGIONS:
A Comparison Guide

	UNIFICATION CHURCH	THE WAY INTERNATIONAL
GOD	The Trinity is the Perfect Man, the Perfect Woman, and the Father, Mr. and Mrs. Moon are the "perfect" couple.	God is one person. The concept of the Trinity is polytheistic.
CHRIST	Jesus is not God; "Jesus attained deity as a man who fulfilled the purpose of creation but by no means can be considered God Himself." Jesus failed in his mission: "Jesus didn't come to be persecuted and die on the cross." "Jesus died before he had a chance to marry and have children." Denial of resurrection: "Jesus wasn't resurrected from the dead in a new body but as a spirit man."	Christ is Son of God but not God the Son. He is eternal as an idea in the foreknowledge of God, receiving his soul from God and his body from Mary. He is the only human who has God as a Father and is therefore sinless. Jesus is temporal and incarnate as we are, yet somehow different.

We have explored some of the questions about cults and the dangers that they may present to society and culture. But for us, today, there is one more essential question. What will it take to involve in the Church each person who is concerned about young people and about constitutional rights in the battle to insure freedom of the mind? For some, the warning has come too late, only after a family member or church member has already been drawn into some insidious "religious" web. "It can't happen to us" is *not* a valid observation. We have been *reacting* to the problem for several years; now is the time to start to *act* in both constructive and legal ways.

FAMILY OF LOVE/ CHILDREN OF GOD	DIVINE LIGHT MISSION	HARE KRISHNA
	"God is everywhere." "God is in our hearts." "God is in Satan." "God is great, but Guru is greater than God, because if you go to Guru, Guru will show you God."	*Hare Krishna* is the highest personality of the Godhead.
Jesus had sexual relationships. Children of God has diverged from its former fairly orthodox teachings of Christ. There is little mention of him now.	Jesus: another *avatar* (personal incarnation of God). "By giving knowledge, Christ made people sinless." The real Christ is within, that is, a secret Christ."	Jesus Christ was a self-actualized soul who came to earth as a great prophet.

	UNIFICATION CHURCH	THE WAY INTERNATIONAL
HOLY SPIRIT	Representative of "Perfect Mother."	Holy Spirit is a synonym for God. The holy spirit is God's gift to man; it is not capable of sinning. A person may activate it with the mind (study Word) or spirit (speak in tongues). "Since God is Holy Spirit, he can give only what he is—holy spirit." Wierwille has envisioned God's Spirit as an impersonal energy which merges with human holy spirit. The believer activates the holy spirit with the Holy Spirit.
SIN	"God had intended Adam and Eve to marry and have perfect children, thereby establishing the Kingdom of Heaven on earth." The Fall: The fruit is sexual knowledge; the sin is the seduction of Eve by Satan.	The Way emphasizes Romans 10:9. Jesus, being perfect man, took man's sins upon himself. He was the proxy for man's sins and died.
REDEMPTION	Man may attain deity if he fulfills the purpose of creation. The Perfect Father must take the Perfect Mother and fulfill the Kingdom of Heaven by having Perfect Children. Christ's death is not essential to redemption. "Jesus failed in his christly mission. His death on the cross was not an essential part of God's plan for redeeming sinful mankind. "Jesus couldn't accomplish the providence of physical salvation because his body was invaded by Satan."	Man is body and soul; therefore, he must receive human holy spirit which was sent at Pentecost. One hears the Word, repents, and is born again. If one hears the Word and understands it with his mind, he will be born again. Wierwille lays a heavy stress on "renewed mind logic" as a part of the conversion process.

FAMILY OF LOVE/ CHILDREN OF GOD	DIVINE LIGHT MISSION	HARE KRISHNA
Members claim a pentecostal spiritual experience in their lives.	"Christ gave the Holy Spirit, which is that knowledge." ". . . (the Holy Spirit is) that supreme energy which is keeping your body alive."	
The whole world is under impending doom. Children of God will rule the world before Christ's return. However, not all Children of God will be saved, only those who survive the time of testing and tribulation.	Divine Light Mission rejects the need for repentance. "Evil is nothing." "Evil is the ignorance of our mind." "Sin is forgiven by meditation."	The matter/spirit dichotomy is present in man, and the spirit is tarnished by the body. "The material atmosphere . . . is called illusion." There is no acknowledgement of sin, divine forgiveness, or grace.
The second coming of Christ is forecast for 1993. A personal confrontation with Christ and acceptance of him was important. Now the stress is work-oriented toward getting money and new disciples. Children of God are taught to pray to God for all things needed, and God will provide.	The way to knowledge is to meditate on the mantra, and thereby to find God in our hearts. We perceive God-consciousness and oneness with the universe (monism).	Each of us should develop Krishna-consciousness, which will lead to greater love for God and man. Man achieves enlightenment by chanting the "holy names of Krishna." The direct love of *Hare Krishna* is the surest way to "burn off ignorance and to attain bliss." ISKON accepts the doctrine of reincarnation. ISKON does not stress union with the absolute, but rather a transcendental love with the personal deity, Krishna.

	UNIFICATION CHURCH	THE WAY INTERNATIONAL
THE BIBLE	"The Bible is not truth itself, but a textbook which teaches truth." The New Testament words of Jesus and the Holy Spirit will lose their light in later times as new truth is revealed. *Divine Principle,* written by Moon himself, resolves the basic questions of life and the universe. The Bible was written by fallen man and can only be decoded by Mr. Moon.	"The Word is as much God as God is God. . . . The Bible says what it means, and means what it says." Wierwille claims his interpretation of scripture is the only accurate one, with "Revelation Knowledge." Paul's prison epistles are adequate for Christians; the Old Testament and Gospels belong to another, past era. The 1611 Authorized Version is used exclusively.
LEADER & HISTORY	Mr. Sun Myung Moon sees himself as the second Advent of Christ; Moon is the Perfect Father, about to fulfill the uncompleted work of Jesus. Building an "ideal race," God has sent him to "put out the fire"; America has one more chance to follow Moon. Born in North Korea in 1920, Moon had his initial vision of Messiahship in 1936. Excommunicated from the Presbyterian Church in 1948 he founded the Unification Church in 1954. *The Divine Principle* was written in 1957; the movement was established in the U.S.A. in 1972.	The president of The Way is Victor Paul Wierwille, who has spoken directly with God. Formerly ordained in a mainline denomination, he studied at the Chicago Divinity School and the Princeton Theological Seminary, and received an honorary doctorate from Pike's Peak in 1948. Wierwille started to teach the "Power for Abundant Living" course in 1953 and established a center for his teaching. In 1957, he resigned his pulpit in favor of an independent ministry; Wierwille probably anticipated being fired because of disciplinary problems on a missionary trip to India.

FAMILY OF LOVE/ CHILDREN OF GOD	DIVINE LIGHT MISSION	HARE KRISHNA
The "Mo Letters" have replaced the Bible as the written authority and the inspired word for today. The Bible is the inspired word for yesterday. There is a hierarchy of publications coming forth from Berg: for the public, first-year sheep, followers, and leaders.	The scriptures are authentic but do not require scientific exegesis since the aim of the Bible is to help one experience "god."	The Vedic scriptures are used exclusively.
Founded by David Berg, who is known as Moses David. "No power in the world can stand against the spirit of David." A spiritualist; he has dead spiritual counselors who give him information. Children of God encourages witchcraft, rebellion, religious prostitution, and immorality. Children of God had its start in southern California when Berg was defrocked and took over a Teen Challenge Center drawing on "Jesus Movement" people for his start. (Berg was formerly in the Christian and Missionary Alliance Church.) His following is organized into seven tribes of Israel.	Guru Maharaj Ji is the incarnation of "god" and is able to give enlightenment to his disciples; he is the second coming of Christ, the "perfect master for today, here to manifest Christ to man. . . . The Perfect Master is not a human being. The Perfect Master is the Living God on this earth. The one and only Perfect Master of this age—the Christ." Divine Light Mission began with Guru's father in North India and Pakistan in the 1920s giving forth the concepts; Divine Light Mission was organized in 1970 to carry on the father's work after his death in 1968.	Krishna is incarnate in various leaders throughout the ages. A transparent representative of God is worshipped. The last incarnation of Krishna was in 1948. This began unbroken chain of disciplic succession to Guru Prabhupada, who came to the U.S. in 1965.

	UNIFICATION CHURCH	**THE WAY INTERNATIONAL**
GROWTH	3 million estimated worldwide. 30,000 Americans with an estimated 2,000–3,000 new membership contacts monthly. Estimated 7,000–10,000 core workers in U.S.A.	There is no claim of membership rolls. In 1976, 683 enrolled at The Way College of Emporia, Kansas; 425 in The Way Missionary Corps. Low estimate of U.S. followers is 20,000 with perhaps 100,000 involved. In recent years, Way has had over 1,000 "WOW Ambassadors" around the country annually.
GOALS	To inform earth that the Messiah has arrived and wants to unify world with Moon as the head. Allegations made that Moon both wants to take over U.S. government and that he is supported by South Korean government. Moon appears to reject democracy and to equate communism with Satan. "God wants America as his base. . . . America has been the chosen defender of God. . . . The whole world is in my hands, and I will conquer and subjugate the world. . . . We must make a new U.N."	To spread God's Word, as interpreted by Dr. Wierwille, who is regarded as modern-day St. Paul by Way followers. Involvement encouraged by adherents in political process, with Constitutional Political Alliance as separate organization to "keep God's Word living in the U.S." C.P.A. aims to get God's leaders into public office. God's leaders, by Way theology, appear to be Way believers mostly.

FAMILY OF LOVE/ CHILDREN OF GOD	DIVINE LIGHT MISSION	HARE KRISHNA
Estimated at 5,000 in 1977, with fewer than 15% in U.S.A. 80 colonies worldwide. Berg's disciples, under their new name, the "Family of Love," are reestablishing themselves in the United States.	Estimated 50,000 in U.S.A. with 20,000 in Europe and Africa. While once strong, the group appears to be fading.	About 7,000 members in U.S.A.
Berg sees world under impending doom. Children of God to evangelize world and rule earth before Jesus comes. Israel will be invaded by Russia, and both Israel and U.S.A. will be defeated, with establishment of world communistic government. Armageddon will take place at Christ's return 7 years later (1993). Moses David (Berg) is to be established as the end-time prophet.	To unite the world in the garland of unity, brotherhood, and love . . . to bring the world out of darkness.	To spread Krishna consciousness in the West. They desire to have an ISKON World Center in Manhattan.

	UNIFICATION CHURCH	**THE WAY INTERNATIONAL**
MIND CONTROL	Mind and sense bombardment is common, with no time alone. Threats of Satan coupled with emotional seduction and sensory deprivation.	Indoctrination techniques known to erase convert's past history, with control exercised over convert to least detail. Post-hypnotic suggestion has been shown with many escapees, through danger of "quick recall" by hypnotic suggestion.
	Pretended agreement with converts coupled with rejection of all negative thoughts; antagonism dwindles to apathy, and finally to acceptance. "I am your brain. . . . What I wish must be your wish." Use of Korean War brainwashing techniques alleged.	
MONEY	Estimated $15 million in property in New York, which is to be the new Garden of Eden. Solicitations brought in $10 million in 1975, according to President of Church. Ex-followers estimate closer to $60 million.	$100.00 tuition for the "Power for Abundant Living" course for over 33 hours of taped lectures. If they met their membership goals, they would raise over $1 million monthly in PFAL tuition alone. Corp program costs member $300 monthly for three years. Budget is not revealed to public; one director was fired for asking about financial arrangements.
	Moon has invested heavily in numerous commercial interests, including a daily New York City newspaper and fishing interests along the American coastline.	
LEGAL PROBLEMS	"Heavenly deception," a common tool in recruiting and soliciting, has prompted many local governments to seek to bar Unification from their communities. These actions have resulted in numerous lawsuits instigated by Unification.	The Way was sued for $296,825 by a quadraplegic who alleges he was defrauded of money for "gift of healing." The Way countersued for $800,000, and the case was settled out of court.
		New York parents have filed suit claiming daughter is brainwashed and constantly harassed by Way members.

FAMILY OF LOVE/ CHILDREN OF GOD	DIVINE LIGHT MISSION	HARE KRISHNA
Constant repetition of biblical passages, out of context, which tell converts to leave family and to obey leaders of Children of God. God will retaliate against those who leave. Some ex-members claim they were not brainwashed. Members are always supervised and told to "follow your shepherd. . . . I love you." Many members have been deprogrammed, with extensive rehabilitation afterwards.	Numerous members have had to go through extensive treatment to regain emotional and intellectual freedom.	Numerous ex-members feel they were not able to act independently of the group's processes. Escapees have been successfully deprogrammed and rehabilitated.
Each individual solicits $100–$300 daily, mostly through sale of "Mo Letters." All possessions to be forsaken, and classes in letter writing held for solicitation from parents. Information form is filled out concerning inheritance, trusts, etc. Individuals receive little financial support from Children of God.	Approximate income is $3 million annually. Each new member is required to fill out a two-page information sheet on assets: trusts, inheritances, stocks, etc.	The Krishnas are extremely aggressive in soliciting at transportation centers, selling magazines, flowers, or buttons to support their "children's work" or other "causes." One enterprise, "Spiritual Skies Incense" nets them over $2 million every year.
Refused in 1972 to appear in court countersuit for disclosure of funds. Most centers and converts moved at that time to Europe and began in 1978 to return to the United States.		In 1976 New York City D.A. investigating finances. Several cases by parents against ISKON for psychological kidnapping; ISKON members also suing parents.

Notes

INTRODUCTION

1. Documentation on file with author.
2. *Life,* 6 September 1971, p. 54.
3. Malnak v. Yogi, 440 F. Supp. 1284 (1977) (Berkeley, Calif.: Spiritual Counterfeits Project, 1978).
4. Documentation on file with author.
5. Walter Martin, *The Kingdom of the Cults* (Minneapolis: Bethany Fellowship, 1965), p. 11.
6. *Gnosticism* derives from the Greek *gnosis,* "knowledge." This school of thought first gained prominence in the second century and had its roots in paganism. "Gnosis" was the supposedly revealed knowledge of God that led to redemption. The gnostics felt that the possession of "knowledge" would rescue "spirtual" men, while "fleshly" men remained unredeemed. Their characteristic world view was of good(everything they stood for) and evil (all else).

CHAPTER 1

1. Ronald Enroth, Edward Ericson, and C. B. Peters, *The Jesus People* (Grand Rapids, Mich.: W. B. Eerdmans, 1972).
2. Matt. 7:16.
3. Acts 9.
4. Documentation on file with author.
5. Ibid.

6. Reported in Ronald Enroth, *Youth, Brainwashing, and the Extremist Cults* (Grand Rapids, Mich.: Zondervan, 1977). p. 173.
7. Henry Brandreth, *Episcopi Vagantes and the Anglican Church* (London: S.P.C.K., 1961), p. 2.
8. Documentation on file with author.
9. Internal Revune Service Code No. 170.
10. Documentation on file with author.
11. Reported in Annatte Daum, ed., *Missionary and Cult Movements,* (New York: Union of American Hebrew Congregations, Department of Interreligious Affairs, 1977).
12. *New York Times,* 24 April 1977, p. 25.
13. Report of the Charity Frauds Bureau of the State of New York, p. 12.
14. Documentation on file with author.
15. Ibid.
16. Matt. 10:36.
17. Documentation on file with author.
18. Ibid.
19. Ibid.
20. Daum, *Missionary and Cult Movements.*
21. Ibid.
22. J. MacCollam, *The Way of Victor Paul Wierwille* (Downers Grove, Ill.: Inter-Varsity Press, 1978).
23. Daum, *Missionary and Cult Movements.*
24. As reported by Carroll Stoner and Jo Anne Parke, *All God's Children* (Radnor, Pa.: Chilton Books, 1977), p. 37, from materials drawn from cult recruitment pamphlet.
25. Malnak v. Yogi.
26. Isa. 55:1ff.
27. Rom. 5:6.

CHAPTER 2

1. Stoner and Parke, *All God's Children,* p. 76.
2. John Clark, Testimony before the Vermont State Legislature.
3. James Monegan, "Free Minds and the Freedom of Religion," unpublished paper, p. 5.
4. Documentation on file with author.
5. Daum, *Missionary and Cult Movements.*
6. Documentation on file with author.
7. Daum, *Missionary and Cult Movements.*

8. Stoner and Parke, *All God's Children*, p. 28.
9. *Los Angeles Times*, 24 July, 1978.

CHAPTER 3

1. Alvin Toffler, *Future Shock* (New York: Random House, 1970).
2. *Psychology Today*, July 1977, p. 39.
3. Marie Winn, *The Plug-In Drug: Television, Children, and the Family* (New York: Bantam Books, 1978).

CHAPTER 4

1. Monegan, *Free Minds*, p. 7.
2. Documentation on file with author.
3. Ibid.
4. Ibid.
5. Richard Delgado, "Religious Totalism: Gentle and Ungentle Persuasion under the First Amendment" (Los Angeles: *Southern California Law Review*, November 1977), citing Robert Lifton, *Thought Reform* (London: Victor Gollancz, 1962).
6. *New York Daily News*, December 1–5, 1975.
7. *People*, 24 July 1978, p. 24.
8. *Montreal Star*, 1 January 1978, letter to the editor.
9. Documentation on file with author.
10. Ibid.
11. *Los Angeles Times*, 9 September 1978, p. II/8.
12. Documentation on file with author.
13. Ibid.
14. *Albany Churchman*, December 1975, p. 12.
15. Daum, *Missionary and Cult Movements*.

CHAPTER 5

1. Stoner and Parke, *All God's Children*, p. xii.
2. Documentation on file with author.
3. Ibid.
4. Ibid.
5. Ibid.
6. Ibid.
7. Ibid.

CHAPTER 6

1. *Jewish Press,* 2 September 1977, p. 41.
2. Ibid.
3. Ibid.
4. Ibid.
5. Nashville *Tennessean,* 19 December 1976, p. 1.
6. Ibid., p. 14.
7. Ibid.
8. Documentation on file with author.
9. "Impact of Cults on Today's Youth," Report of the California Senate Subcommittee on Children and Youth, 24 August 1974, pp. 29–31.
10. Ibid., pp. 66–67.
11. Ibid., p. 72.
12. Ibid., p. 71.
13. Ibid., p. 76.

CHAPTER 7

1. Documentation on file with author. Quoted in "Information Kit" distributed by Union of American Hebrew Congregations.
2. *People.*
3. *Master Speaks.* Quoted in *Mission and Cult Movements.*
4. V. P. Wierwille, *Jesus Christ Is Not God* (New Knoxville, Ohio: The American Christian Press, 1975), p. 4.
5. Statement of the Faith and Order Commission of the National Council of Churches.
6. James A. Rudin. Quoted in *Missions and Cult Movement,* Union of American Hebrew Congregations.
7. Lifton, *Thought Reform.*
8. J. A. C. Brown, *Techniques of Mind Control and Persuasion* (New York: Peloquin Books), p. A604.
9. *People.*
10. Frederick L. Marcuse, *Hypnotism: Fact and Fiction* (New York: Penguin Books, 1959).
11. Marvin Karlins and Herbert Abelson, *Persuasion: How Opinions and Attitudes are Changed* (New York: Springer, 1970), p. 1.
12. Flo Conway and Jim Siegelman, *Snapping: America's Epidemic*

of Sudden Personality Change (New York: J. B. Lippincott, 1978), p. 48.

13. Documentation on file with author.
14. Clark, Testimony.
15. Dusty Sklar, *Gods and Beasts: The Nazis and the Occult* (New York: Thomas Crowell, 1977).
16. Documentation on file with author.
17. Ibid.
18. Ibid.
19. Ibid.
20. "The Phil Donahue Show," interview with former cult programmer and cult lawyer.
21. "The Rene Baxter Newsletter," quoted in *The Edifier,* vol. 1, no. 3 (St. Mary's, Ohio: Edify Associates).
22. *Truth Is My Sword,* a report on the Frasier Committee Investigations.
23. *Master Speaks,* quoted in Union of American Hebrew Congregations.

CHAPTER 8

1. Stoner and Parke, *All God's Children,* p. 162, quoting Richard Delgado.
2. Documentation on file with author.
3. Ibid.
4. American Civil Liberties Union, "Philadelphia Report," (July 1976), p. 6.
5. Documentation on file with author.
6. Clark, Testimony.
7. "Deprogramming: Documenting the Issue," prepared for the American Civil Liberties Union and the Toronto School of Theology Conferences on Religious Deprogramming, p. Ig/37.
8. Richard Delgado. "Religious Totalism," p. 92.
9. American Civil Liberties Union, IIc/77.
10. *How to Survive Deprogramming.* Pamphlet on file with author.
11. Documentation on file with author.
12. Ibid.
13. *The Living Church,* 6 August 1978, p. 7.
14. American Civil Liberties Union, p. Id/17.
15. Ibid.
16. Clark, Testimony.

17. Documentation on file with author.
18. Resolution on Missionaries and Deprogramming, adopted November 1977 by the Biennial Meeting of the Union of American Hebrew Congregations.
19. Documentation on file with author.
20. Ibid.
21. Ibid.
22. Ibid.

CHAPTER 9

1. "A Bill for Establishing Religious Freedom," italicized in the original and deleted by the Virginia General Assembly in 1779, prior to adoption in 1786.
2. Delgado, "Religious Totalism," p. 7.
3. *Washington Star,* 21 April 1977, p. A12.
4. Documentation on file with author.
5. *People.*
6. "Challenge of the Cults" (Philadelphia: Jewish Community Relations Council), p. 40.
7. Monegan, *Free Minds,* p. 5.
8. Quoted in Ruebhausen and Brin, *Privacy and Behavioral Research,* 65 Col. L. Rev. 1184 (1965).
9. "Challenge of the Cults," p. 41.
10. Documentation on file with author.
11. *Episcopal Clerical Directory, 1977; Episcopal Church Annual, 1978.*
12. *The Courier* (Germantown, Pa), 16 March 1977. See also *Courier-Post* (Camden, NJ), 7 July 1977.
13. *Philadelphia Bulletin,* 17 September 1977.
14. *American Civil Liberties Union* p. IVj/195.
15. Delgado, "Religious Totalism," pp. 10f.
16. Ibid., p. 57.
17. Eric A. Schuppen, unpublished paper.
18. Ibid.
19. *American Civil Liberties Union Reports,* "Deprogramming," January 1978, p. 8.
20. Delgado, "Religious Totalism," p. 59.
21. Harvey Cox, quoted in *Cleveland Plain Dealer,* 22 October, 1977, p. B30.
22. Seattle *Post Intelligencer,* 12 December 1974, p. D18.

23. Leslie Weiss v. Theodore Patrick, Jr. alias John Doe, v. Albert Turner, alias Richard Doe, C.A. No. 75-0223 (U.S. District Court for Rhode Island, 1978).
24. Los Angeles *Herald Examiner*, 22 June 1978.
25. *Liberty*, magazine, March–April 1975, p. 13.
26. Statement by Dean Kelly in *Deprogramming: Documenting the Issue*, Addenda p. 21.
27. Benjamin Cardoza, *Paradoxes of Legal Science* (New York: Columbia University Press, 1928), p. 104.
28. *Deprogramming: Documenting the Issue*, p. IVh/163.

CHAPTER 10

1. Isa. 55:1–2; Rom. 5:14–18.

CHAPTER 11

1. I Cor. 12–14.
2. Stoner and Parke, *All God's Children*, p. 227.

Bibliography

The following resources represent various viewpoints concerning new religious groups. The inclusion of any religious leader or religious group in this bibliography does not necessarily represent the judgment of the author that a particular group might be classified as a "cult."

ARTICLES

Baldwin, Frank. "Korea Lobby." *Christianity and Crisis*, 19 July 1976, pp. 162–188.

Black, David. "Why Kids Join Cults." *Woman's Day*, February 1977.

Chandler, R. "Fighting Cults: The Tucson Tactic." *Christianity Today*, 4 February 1977.

"The Children of God, Disciples of Deception." *Christianity Today*, 18 February 1977.

Cornell, G. W. "Those Guru Cults: Religion or Exploitation?" *Reader's Digest*, February 1976, pp. 96–100.

Cowley, Susan Cheever, and Shim, Jae Hoon. "Many Moons." *Newsweek*, 26 April 1976, pp. 94–95.

Cox, Harvey. "Teens and the Religious Revival." *Parents' Magazine*, February 1978, pp. 52ff.

"The Darker Side of Sun Moon," *Time*, 14 June 1976, p. 48.

Delgado, Richard. "Religious Totalism: Gentle and Ungentle Persuasion under the First Amendment." *Southern California Law Review*, November 1977.

"Deprogramming: The Cults Fight Back." *Christianity Today*, 17 June 1977, pp. 36–37.

Edwards, Charles H. "How I Rescued My Son from the Moonies." *Medical Economics*, November 1976, pp. 73–80.

Ericson, Edward, and MacPherson, Paul. "The Deception of the Children of God." *Christianity Today*, 20 July 1973, pp. 14–20.

Footlick, Jerrold K., et. al. "Parents v. Moonies." *Newsweek*, 25 April 1977, p. 83.

Gunther, Max. "Brainwashing: Persuasion by Propaganda." *Today's Health*, February 1976, pp. 15ff.

Kempton, Sally. "Hanging Out with the Guru." *New York*, 12 April 1976.

MacCollam, Joel A. "The Way: Who They Are and What They Believe." *Christian Herald*, November 1977, p. 53ff.

——. "The Unification Church: Behind a Smiling Face, a History of Broken Hearts, Broken Lives, and Broken Homes." *The Living Church*, 12 December 1976, pp. 8–9.

——. "Cults and their Victims: The Case for Deprogramming." *The Living Church*, 24 July 1977.

——. "Cults and Young Adults." *Aware*, vol. III, supp. 2, 1977.

McCready, William C. "Youth and Religious Cults: A Search for Meaning or Exploitation of the Young?" *Youth*, February 1977, pp. 3–13.

"Mad about Moon." *Time*, 10 November 1975, p. 44.

Marvin, Peter. "The New Narcissism." *Harpers*. October 1975.

Matthews, Arthur H. "Meeting Moon at the Monument." *Christianity Today*, 8 October 1976, pp. 59–62.

Meether, Arthur, J. L. "Combating the Cults." *Lutheran Standard*, 15 February 1977, pp. 12–13.

Montagno, Margaret, *et al.* "Is Deprogramming Legal? *Newsweek*, 21 February 1977, p. 44.

Peerman, Dean. "Korean Moonshine." *Christian Century*, 4 December 1974, pp. 1139–41.

Plowman, Edward E. "Deprogramming: A Right to Rescue?" *Christianity Today*, 7 May 1976, pp. 38–39.

Rasmussen, Mark. "How Sun Myung Moon Lures America's Children." *McCall's*, September 1976, pp. 102ff.

"Religious Cults: Newest Magnet for Youth." *U.S. News and World Report*, 14 June 1976.

Rice, Berkeley. "Honor Thy Father Moon." *Psychology Today*, January 1976.

124693

——. "The Pull of Sun Moon." *New York Times Magazine,* 20 May 1976, pp. 8ff.

Robbins, T. "Deprogramming the Brainwashed: Even a Moonie Has Rights." *Nation,* 26 February 1977.

Robbins, T. and Anthony, D D. "New Religious, Families, and Brainwashing." *Society,* May 1978, pp. 77–83.

Sage, Wayne. "The War on the Cults." *Human Behavior,* October 1977, pp. 40–49.

Stenzel, James. "Rev. Moon and His Bicentennial Blitz." *Christianity and Crisis,* 19 July 1976, pp. 173–175.

"To Another Planet—and Back." *Time,* 14 June 1976, p. 50.

Woodward, Kenneth L., *et al.* "Life with Father Moon." *Newsweek,* 14 June 1976, pp. 60–66.

Woodward, Kenneth L., and Woodward, Elizabeth. "Why Are Teens Turning to Religion?" *Seventeen,* July 1975.

BOOKLETS AND BOOKS

Bhaktivedanta, A. C. *The Bhagavad Gita as It Is.* Los Angeles: Bhaktivedanta Press, 1968, 1972.

Brill, Abraham. *Basic Principles of Psychoanalysis.* New York: Washington Square Press, 1968.

Brown, James A. C. *Techniques of Persuasion.* New York: Penguin, 1963.

Cohen, Daniel. *The New Believers: Young Religion in America.* New York: M. Evans, 1975.

Daner, Francine Jeanne. *The American Children of Krsna.* New York: Holt, Rinehart & Winston, 1976.

Daum, Annatte, ed. *Missionary and Cult Movements.* New York: Union of American Hebrew Congregations, 1977.

Enroth, Ronald M. *Youth, Brainwashing, and the Extremist Cults.* Grand Rapids, Mich.: Zondervan, 1977.

Enroth, Ronald M.; Ericson, Edward E.; and Peters. C. B. *The Jesus People: Old-Time Religion in the Age of Aquarius.* Grand Rapids, Mich.: Wm. B. Eerdmans, 1972.

Evans, Christopher R. *Cults of Unreason.* New York: Dell, 1973.

Fair, Charles. *The New Nonsense: The End of the Rational Consequences. New York:* Simon & Schuster, 1974.

Greenfield, Robert. Spiritual Supermarket. New York: Saturday Review Press, 1975.

Kanter, Rosabeth Moss. *Commitment and Community*. Cambridge, Mass.: Harvard University Press, 1972.

MacCollam, Joel A. *The Way of Victor Paul Wierwille*. Downers Grove, Ill.: Inter-Varsity Press, 1978.

Marcuse, Frederick L. *Hypnotism: Fact and Fiction*. New York: Penguin Books, 1959.

Martin, Walter R. *Kingdom of the Cults*. Minneapolis: Bethany Fellowship, 1965.

Patrick, Ted, and Dulack, Tom. *Let Our Children Go!* New York: E. P. Dutton, 1976.

Report of the Charity Frauds Bureau of the State of New York on the Children of God. Albany, N.Y.: The Attorney General's Office, 1974.

Sargent, William. *Battle for the Mind: The Psychology of Conversion and Brainwashing*. New York: Harper & Row, 1959.

Sontag, Frederick. *Sun Myung Moon and the Unification Church*. Nashville, Tenn.: Abingdon Press, 1977.

Sparks, Jack. *The Mindbenders*. Nashville, Tenn.: Thomas Nelson, 1977.

Stoner, Carroll, and Parke, Jo Anne. *All God's Children: The Cult Experience–Salvation or Slavery*. Radnor, Pa.: Chilton Books, 1977.

TM in Court: The Complete Text of the Federal Court's Opinion in the Case of Malnak v. Maharishi Mahesh Yogi. Berkeley, Calif.: Spiritual Counterfeits Project, 1978.

Toffler, Alvin. *Future Shock*. New York: Random House, 1970.

Wallenstedt, Alan. *The Way: A Biblical Analysis*. Berkeley, Calif.: Spiritual Counterfeits Project, 1976.

Whiteside, Elena S. *The Way: Living in Love*. New Knoxville, Ohio: American Christian Press, 1972.

Wierwille, Victor Paul. *Jesus Christ Is Not God*. New Knoxville, Ohio: American Christian Press, 1972.

Yamamoto, J. Isamu. *The Moon Doctrine*. Downers Grove, Ill.: Inter-Varsity Press, 1976.

———. *The Puppet Master*. Downers Grove, Ill.: Inter-Varsity Press, 1977.